Ideas about Agriculture in the Political Economy of Japan

Ideas about Agriculture in the Political Economy of Japan:

The Foundation of the Nation?

By

James M. Brady

Cambridge
Scholars
Publishing

Ideas about Agriculture in the Political Economy of Japan:
The Foundation of the Nation?

By James M. Brady

This book first published 2021

Cambridge Scholars Publishing

Lady Stephenson Library, Newcastle upon Tyne, NE6 2PA, UK

British Library Cataloguing in Publication Data
A catalogue record for this book is available from the British Library

ISBN (10): 1-5275-6211-5
ISBN (13): 978-1-5275-6211-0

To Ani

"To take care of the roots and to keep the branches under control, this is the principle taught by the sages of old. The root is agriculture; the branches industry and commerce."

—Ogyū Sorai, philosopher (1666-1728)

"In our country the words 'agriculture is the foundation of the nation' have virtually become the racial faith of the Yamato people."

—Ishiguro Tada'ashi, agriculture minister (1884-1960)

"Our country's agriculture and rural villages, together with their function in supplying food that is indispensable to the life of the Japanese people, through their activities perform such roles as preserving the national land, and are indeed the 'foundation of the nation.'"

—Foreword to the *Basic Plan for Food, Agriculture and Rural Villages*, March 2020

TABLE OF CONTENTS

LIST OF TABLES

LIST OF FIGURES

List of Abbreviations and Terms

amakudari	post-retirement bureaucrats who find second careers in the same sector, often in *gaikaku dantai*
APEC	Asia Pacific Economic Cooperation
BSE	bovine spongiform encephalopathy
CGE	Computable General Equilibrium (economic model)
CPTPP	Comprehensive and Progressive agreement for Trans Pacific Partnership, the 11-member successor to the TPP
CSE	Consumer Support Estimate
DPJ	Democratic Party of Japan
EPA	Economic Partnership Agreement
FAO	Food and Agriculture Organization of the United Nations
FTA	Free Trade Agreement
gaikaku dantai	semi-governmental organisations
GATT	General Agreement on Tariffs and Trade
JA	Japan Agriculture, English name of *Nōkyō*
JA-Zenchū	peak political body of JA, known as the 'Central Union of Agricultural Cooperatives' in English
JA-Zennoh	peak marketing & supply body of JA, known as 'National Federation of Agricultural Cooperatives' in English
JEUEPA	Japan-EU Economic Partnership Agreement
Keidanren	the Japan Business Federation
LDP	Liberal Democratic Party
MAFF	Ministry of Agriculture, Forestry and Fisheries
nōhonshugi	agricultural fundamentalism, a body of thought
nōhonshugisha	proponent of agricultural fundamentalism
Nōkyō	agricultural cooperative group, known as JA in English
Nōkyō gi'in	Diet members who previously worked for *Nōkyō*
Norinchūkin	banking arm of *Nōkyō*
nōrin gi'in	'agriculture and forestry' Diet members
nōson gi'in	'farm politicians' or rural Diet members
nōrin zoku	'agricultural tribe' politicians
PSE	Producer Support Estimate

OECD	Organisation for Economic Cooperation and Development
RCEP	Regional Comprehensive Economic Partnership
TPP	Trans Pacific Partnership, a 12-member trade agreement from which the United States subsequently withdrew
SCAP	Supreme Commander for the Allied Powers
satoyama-no-fūkei	Japan's traditional village scenery
sei'iki	'sacred' or 'sanctuary' categories in trade negotiations, covering rice, beef and pork, wheat, sugar, and dairy
Uruguay Round	eighth round of the GATT/WTO negotiations, 1986-94
WTO	World Trade Organisation

PREFACE

The thirteenth-century Japanese Zen master Dōgen wrote,

> Enlightenment is like the moon reflected on the water.
> The moon does not get wet nor is the water broken.
> Although its light is wide and great,
> The moon is reflected in a puddle even an inch wide.
> *The whole moon and the entire sky*
> *Are reflected on one dewdrop in the grass.*

The image of seeing the vastness of the night sky reflected in a single drop of water, carefully observed, is one that frequently came to mind, the longer I examined the topic of agriculture in Japan and saw so much of the country's culture and history and identity reflected therein. The beginnings of this book, however, lie somewhere much less poetic—in studies of the economics of Japan's trade policy options in the late 2000s. As numerous models at that time demonstrated, the potential welfare gains from trade liberalisation in the context of a U.S-Japan or ASEAN+3 free trade agreement were great, and a greater openness to trade would surely bring a welcome stimulus for an economy then enduring a second 'lost decade' of growth.

The failure by successive Japanese governments to pick this low-hanging fruit was puzzling to me, particularly because the main stumbling block in international trade negotiations seemed to be the protection of Japan's small and declining agricultural sector. Surely a dwindling band of elderly rice farmers couldn't impede the future of one of the world's great economies? Still youthful and optimistic, I wondered whether some well-designed academic research could help solve the problem and open the way for freer trade and stronger economic growth.

Finding standard economic explanations of this agricultural conundrum to be simplistic and unsatisfying, I turned instead to the great corpus of work by the political scientist Aurelia George Mulgan, the leading Western scholar in the field. Her accounts of the interest-based political interactions of JA, MAFF, and politicians were comprehensive, cogent, and convincing—

if infuriating for what they revealed about the power of sectional interests. This literature gave an insightful exposition of the political constraints on the Japanese government in international trade negotiations.

Yet even this approach didn't seem to explain one important fact that I observed over and over in my surroundings in Osaka—that the Japanese people with whom I discussed my research were well-informed about the costs and trade-offs, and still fully supportive of an agricultural policy regime that raised their food bills and limited their consumption choices. Above all, they would say, they simply couldn't imagine a Japan that didn't produce rice. I found this view to be as common with economics professors as with students and salary-people. The pursuit of self-interest may have been shaping outcomes at the elite policy actor level, but something else was clearly going on with voters, who were also consumers and taxpayers.

Eventually, I discovered that there was already a solid body of communicative literature from other disciplines that helped explain these protectionist attitudes, such as Emiko Ohnuki-Tierney's wonderful book *Rice As Self*. My research task gradually evolved from trying to explain how best Japanese policymakers should reform their country (a well-trodden path among foreign scholars and pundits), to trying to fully understand the reasons *why* Japanese citizens valued their agricultural sector and their rice so deeply, and to articulate those reasons within a political economy framework. It was the start of a fascinating journey through the highways and byways of Japanese history, political thought, cultural anthropology, and media studies, with various detours (both intellectual and geographical) along the way.

The key realisation was that in essence this was a conflict of *ideas*—ideas that arose from their own historical and cultural contexts, developed and were transmitted over time, and that now compete to shape the policy preferences of individuals. Though it may sound almost commonplace to say today, economic welfare is at root but one idea among many, albeit the dominant idea so strongly privileged in policy discourse the world over. As a now-recovering economist, it required me to go back almost to the very beginnings of Micro-economics 101 to realise the specific set of unspoken assumptions embedded in mainstream economic analyses, and then to operationalise a new approach to ideas within a framework that met the rigours of social science and bridged the various disciplines within which I was now working. In presenting my argument about the role of ideas about agriculture in the chapters that follow, I hope I have been successful in drawing together the compelling evidence that arises from various sources and academic fields (as well as my own original research), and in articulating it in a way that will satisfy economists and political scientists alike.

******

The academic debts incurred throughout the long arc of this research are too great ever to be repaid, but I should at least try to number them. The project would never have been completed without the unfailing support and guidance of Hiro Lee and Virgil Hawkins at Osaka University, Shigeyuki Abe of Doshisha University, and the late Toshihiko Hayashi at the Asia Pacific Institute of Research. Aurelia George Mulgan at the University of New South Wales-ADFA generously read the manuscript at various stages, and offered comments that improved both the text and my understanding of the topic immensely.

At the School of International Public Policy at Osaka University, Toshiya Hoshino, Haruko Satoh, and Naho Hashimoto also provided valuable assistance. At the Modern East Asia Research Centre at Leiden University, Lindsay Black and Bryce Wakefield were my academic compasses when I got lost, and Chris Goto Jones and Katarzyna Cwiertka also gave valuable input on key chapters.

This book also owes much to my time at the Asia Pacific Institute of Research (APIR) in Osaka, where as a research fellow (*kenkyū'in*) I was given every opportunity to learn more about contemporary agricultural policy and to speak with everyone from leading policy specialists in Tokyo to muddy-booted farmers in remote mountain valleys. Hideo Miyahara, Yoshihisa Inada, Mampei Hayashi, Mitsuhiro Okano, Yusuke Kinoshita, Hideo Murakami, Akihiro Shima, Toshiharu Tsuji, Machiko Fujita, Josh Matsukawa, and Miles Neale helped at many points and in many ways. The public opinion survey that appears in Chapter 7 Section 3 was originally undertaken as part of an APIR research project, and appears here with kind permission.

Latterly, Robert Eldridge was pivotal in motivating and helping me find a publisher, and giving excellent feedback on the manuscript. Emma Dalton and Graham Leonard also kindly read drafts and provided many useful comments. Adam Rummens and colleagues at Cambridge Scholars Publishing were thoroughly professional and expeditious in turning the manuscript into a book. For any errors that may remain in the text, I am fully responsible.

Finally, my love to my parents, Breda and Jim, who encouraged and supported me throughout, though I travelled on such an unexpected path; to Julie, Tappy, and Fred, for bringing joy in these challenging times; and most of all to Ani, for everything so far, and everything still to come.

Baltimore, USA
December 2020

CHAPTER 1

INTRODUCTION: THE PUZZLE OF AGRICULTURAL POLICY IN JAPAN

In a chronically low-growth economy with high debt and deficit burdens, why would a government maintain policies of agricultural support and protection that benefit only a tiny proportion of the population yet impose significant costs on the entire society? Moreover, among the non-farm population for whom material welfare and consumer choice are both reduced by such policies, why would an enduring majority implicitly or explicitly support their continuation, as evidenced through voting behaviour, food preferences, and public opinion surveys? These are two central questions at the heart of the puzzle of the political economy of agriculture in Japan, where a sector employing 3.4% of the labour force and producing only 1.2% of GDP maintains a position of privilege that far exceeds its economic importance in one of the world's most advanced industrialised nations.

By most measures, it appears to be an extremely irrational situation. Farmers are supported by a complex and expensive system of subsidies related to crop production and land use, and are protected from international competition by a bewildering array of import tariffs, tariff rate quotas, and other barriers. The direct economic costs of these policies are borne by taxpayers through government subsidies to farmers and by consumers through food prices well above world market rates. The indirect costs are perhaps higher still, and it has been estimated that Japan could increase its annual economic welfare by an amount equivalent to 2% of GDP or more annually through greater liberalisation of trade in agriculture and other sectors (Lee and Itakura, 2014). A government study also found that high prices for produce were contributing to consumers eating less fruit, vegetables, and seafood,[1] suggesting that the current policy regime may be damaging to the physical health as well as the economic welfare of the nation.

Agricultural protectionism has long been a contentious issue in Japan's international relations too, from escalating bilateral frictions with the United States over beef and oranges in the 1970s and 1980s to the recent mega trade agreement negotiations like the Trans Pacific Partnership (TPP) and Japan-EU Economic Partnership Agreement. The very low level of agricultural concessions made by Japan in trade agreements until 2014[2] speaks to the ongoing bipartisan political support for the farming sector. This protectionist posture prevailed despite pressure from Japan's wealthy multinational firms and business federations, whose financial interests are served by greater trade liberalisation. In short, support for farmers has come with high costs for the Japanese government domestically and internationally for almost half a century.

Traditional accounts of the prevalence of protectionism in the political economy of agriculture in Japan tend to focus heavily on the policy outcomes of self-interest pursuit by farmers and the agricultural lobby, bureaucrats, and politicians and parties, with relatively little focus on why so many voters and consumers not only tolerate but actually endorse the policy regime. This study offers a fresh perspective on the puzzle of agricultural policy in Japan by examining the role of ideas in shaping policy preferences. It does so by considering three distinct aspects: the origins of ideas as articulated by agrarian thinkers in early modern and modern Japan, the development of ideas in major agricultural policy debates in the postwar era, and the most influential ideas about agriculture among voters and consumers as recorded in public opinion survey data from the 1970s until the present day. Taken together, these elements offer substantial evidence that ideas are an essential but heretofore overlooked factor that more fully explains the political economy of agriculture in Japan, and one that can serve as a useful compass for orienting the future direction of agricultural policy during a time of multiple major crises.

1.1 Explaining the Paradox

Why have the interests of ageing paddy-farmers prevailed over those of urban voters, consumers, and tax-payers in postwar Japan? According to the leading Western scholar of the politics of Japanese agriculture, Aurelia George Mulgan, "a complete explanation for relatively high levels of agricultural support and protection in Japan requires a complex multifactorial account of the diverse political, historical, economic, bureaucratic, *ideological* and other elements involved" (Mulgan, 2000: 1; emphasis added). Scholars from a variety of disciplines have attempted to follow these interwoven threads, but political economy accounts have focused primarily on two factors: interests and institutions.

One strand of literature focuses on structural interests of individuals maximising their own economic welfare. Traditional political economy approaches posit that agricultural protection is a result of competition between groups of individuals in the context of economic growth and structural change,[3] due to rapid industrial development and the resultant decline of comparative advantage in agriculture as experienced by Japan (and also South Korea and Taiwan) in the twentieth century (e.g. Anderson and Hayami, 1986; Hayami, 1988). These studies offer deductively-derived models rooted in microeconomic theory, in which individuals weigh information and then make rational choices to maximise personal economic welfare. However, this literature lacks predictive power (on its own terms), for example in failing to explain why protectionism has continued past the threshold of 3-4% of GDP or 4-5% of the male labour force (Honma, 1993) when it was predicted to decline. Moreover, factors outside material interests are not analysed in any meaningful way, and many assumptions in the models are inconsistent with the historical record in Japan.

A second strand of literature focuses on the interplay of interests and institutions. These political science approaches to Japan's agricultural sector emphasise such aspects as the agriculture lobby's organisational coherence and influence, the agricultural ministry's interventionist tendencies, biases within the electoral system, and the diffuse nature of policymaking power in Tokyo (e.g. Mulgan, 2000; 2006; 2015; Horiuchi and Saito, 2010; Solis, 2017). As with the structuralist approach, self-interest pursuit is again central, though political scientists analyse group behaviours as well as individuals, and institutional and political outcomes as well as simple material welfare.[4] However, though interest groups and institutions are treated in detail, other explanatory variables like ideas are given relatively little consideration in these studies.

A third approach focuses on policy preferences of groups or individuals that diverge from their assumed economic interests. The political scientist Steven Vogel (1999) argued that Japanese consumer *groups* have distinct preferences and discount price as a factor in making both political and economic decisions, noting that consumer groups fought vigorously against

U.S. pressure for agricultural liberalisation in the 1980s on the grounds that it would undermine food self-sufficiency, increase the risk of contamination or disease, and threaten farmers' livelihoods. Vogel posits that Japanese *consumers* may also discount price relative to other concerns such as environmental protection, social stability, and fairness in competition, possibly influenced by modern Japan's historical experience, in which governments sought to convince consumers to sacrifice short-term interests like lower prices in favour of national goals such as economic growth, military strength, and postwar recovery.

Economists have also examined material interest-divergent behaviours. A behavioural economics study in which Japanese consumers were primed with visual stimuli about their roles as producers or consumers found no effect for consumer-role priming but a stronger opposition to food imports among producer role-primed subjects (Naoi and Kume, 2011). This was particularly strong among those who felt job insecurity themselves, resulting in a "coalition of losers." Another study of attitudes to proposed trade liberalisation through the TPP found that factors shaping opposition to liberalisation included uncertainty about possible outcomes and distributional effects, and a highly organised political coalition of potential losers (Naoi and Urata, 2013).

In terms of trade policy preferences more broadly, a sizeable economics literature exists to explain variance in popular sentiment in many countries towards free trade in spite of the demonstrable welfare gains. In addition to factors such as educational attainment, skill level, and trade exposure of one's employment sector, non-economic factors such as values, identities, and attachments have also been identified as important explanatory variables (e.g. Mayda and Rodrik, 2005). In the United States, "sociotropic" concerns about the impact of liberalisation on the economy as a whole, rather than simply on one's own job, were also found to be a factor shaping consumer attitudes towards liberalisation. (Mansfield and Mutz, 2009).

Fourth, another set of studies have explained the agricultural policy regime in Japan in terms of the broader resonance of agriculture in society. Based on ethnographic interviews of rice farmers and others, Freiner (2019, 2) concludes that "rice is intimately connected to notions of what it means to be Japanese… both in the national consciousness and in policy." In this view, the current agricultural regime is about more than bureaucratic self-preservation and entrenched interests; it is also about "the Japanese nation-state itself" (Freiner, 2019, 8). Regarding Japan's fisheries policy regime,

Barclay and Epstein (2013) argue that the idea of government intervention to provide food for the nation is an essential element of the basic conception of the role of the modern state. These authors contend that the idea of food security resonates so strongly in Japan because it mobilises sentiment related to both sovereignty (securing territory) and Michel Foucault's idea of 'governmentality' (the government's 'biopower' role of intervening in the economy to enhance the lives of citizens). Thus, while the explanatory importance of ideas has been overlooked in the two core strands of literature focused on the political economy of Japanese agriculture, ideas have been explored to a limited extent in other literatures in both economics and political science.

There are a number of reasons to more deeply explore ideas as an explanatory variable shaping policy preferences in the political economy of Japanese agriculture. First, the role of ideas in policymaking has its own extensive literature in various subfields of political science, including foreign policymaking (e.g. Goldstein and Keohane, 1993) and macroeconomic policymaking (e.g. Hall, 1993), and has also been examined in new approaches within mainstream political economy (e.g. Rodrik, 2014; Mukand and Rodrik, 2018). Second, the role of ideas in agricultural policy has been analysed for other major economies like the United States and the European Union (e.g. Goldstein, 1989; Coleman et al., 1997; Skogstad, 1998). Third, ideational aspects relating to the cultural and social importance of agriculture in Japan have been examined extensively in other academic disciplines, including cultural anthropology (e.g. Ohnuki-Tierney, 1993) and history (e.g. Havens, 1974; Gluck, 1987). Fourth, the public policy discourse in Japan often explicitly articulates ideas about the special importance of agriculture, such as descriptions of five categories of agricultural products as *sei'iki* or 'sacred' items[5] in negotiations.

Given these reasons, a more detailed examination of ideational factors in the case of agricultural policy in Japan seems long overdue. The present study fills this gap in the literature and seeks to better explain the paradox of voters and consumers supporting economic welfare-reducing policies by focusing on the role of ideas as a significant explanatory variable in the political economy of agriculture in Japan.

1.2 The Theory

What is an idea in the context of political economy, and how are ideas used analytically? Definitions and usage can vary considerably, as Chapter 4 discusses in detail. Ideas can be studied either as dependent variables that are used instrumentally, strategically, and often cynically by political actors to achieve their goals, or as independent variables that have inherent meaning for actors who truly believe in them. Among scholars who adopt the latter approach and take ideas seriously as an independent variable, rational choice theorists consider ideas to be beliefs held by individuals, which can be world views, principled beliefs, or causal beliefs. Historical institutionalists take ideas to be world views or interpretive frameworks. Organisational institutionalist scholars of domestic politics and constructivists in international relations theory, meanwhile, study ideas as cultural norms.

In utilising ideas for analysis, there are ontological issues to address, such as the relationship between ideas and material interests—are they actually distinct entities, and if so does that distinction exist externally as a fact in the world or internally as a mental construct? Likewise, there are epistemological debates, such as the causality debate regarding whether ideas mechanistically determine a belief or action (as rational choice theorists and many Marxist scholars hold), or logically or conceptually enable it.

The present study begins from a position of taking ideas to be causal beliefs and guides for action. Ideas are understood here as mental constructs that exist within the mind of an individual to suggest either descriptive causal connections about how the world does work or normative causal connections about how it should work. Epistemologically, the study is based on a constituent logic, that ideas provide the conditions to shape beliefs (rather than mechanistically determining belief outcomes). Ontologically, it adopts a position of analytic duality, that the distinction between ideas and material interests exists only in the mind rather than externally. Stated in its simplest formulation, material interests are a sub-set of ideas, and ideas are internal causal beliefs that provide the conditions to shape an individual's beliefs about the external world.

From that theoretical foundation, the central contention of this study is that *ideas are an important independent variable shaping the policy preferences of individuals towards agriculture and agricultural policy in Japan.* It follows that any explanation of the political economy of agriculture will be more complete if it accounts for the role of ideas. It will be argued that voters in Japan see agriculture in complex, multifaceted ways, and as different and special compared with other sectors of the economy. These diverse ideas about agriculture and its role in society shape policy preferences. For these reasons, an enduring majority of voters actively support or implicitly consent to the government protecting the agricultural sector because of its perceived value to them personally and to Japanese society generally in multiple ways, even if protecting agriculture reduces an individual's own material welfare as a taxpayer and food consumer.

Seven distinct types of ideas about agriculture will be explored as explanatory variables, as follows:

(1) ideas about agriculture as a normal part of the economy and business;
(2) ideas about agriculture as having a significant role in Japan's history and culture;
(3) ideas about agriculture related to societal welfare, such as income equality;
(4) ideas about agriculture related to national security, broadly understood, such as food self-sufficiency;[6]
(5) ideas about agriculture related to health and food safety;
(6) ideas about agriculture related to the environment; and
(7) ideas about agriculture related to other reasons that are non-economic in nature, in the sense of not primarily linked to economic welfare concerns.[7]

These ideas will be considered in three contexts: (1) historical strands of political thought relating to agriculture in early modern and modern Japan; (2) postwar policy debates about agriculture in the national press; and (3) contemporary views of agriculture among voters, as expressed through public opinion surveys.

This is an interdisciplinary work that draws on data and studies from a range of disciplines, including political science, economics, history, and cultural anthropology. The methodology aims at cross-disciplinary compatibility, such that data from various disciplines are utilised consistent with a mainstream political economy framework for policy preferences. In particular, ideas (distinct from interests and institutions) are considered in terms of their effects in shaping the policy preferences of individuals, who are considered in terms of their roles as voters, and also as consumers and taxpayers. This individual-level analysis is an important methodological difference with traditional political science approaches that focus on processes and outcomes for policy actors such as interest groups, bureaucrats, and politicians.

1.3 The Structure

The book proceeds as follows. Chapter 2 details the economic and political costs and benefits of Japan's agricultural policy regime at both the domestic and international levels, offering empirical data and numerical estimates where possible. These costs and benefits are then summarised in a political economy balance sheet.

Chapters 3 and 4 develop the theoretical basis for an ideational approach to studying the political economy of agriculture in Japan. Given the apparent economic irrationality of such costly, welfare-reducing policies, Chapter 3 considers the issue of rationality in public policy making and excavates the embedded assumptions of welfare-based economic analyses. Chapter 4 surveys four existing strands of political science and political economy literature that focus on the nexus of ideas and policy, imagines how each of these would explain the case of Japanese agriculture, and outlines an original conceptual framework for how ideas relate to values and policy preferences in a society.

Chapters 5, 6, and 7 apply this new ideational approach to the study of the political economy of agriculture in Japan. Chapter 5 examines ideas about agriculture in modern Japan among philosophers, policymakers, and notable popular thinkers by tracing the development of ideas associated with the body of agrarian thought known as *nōhonshugi*, from the Meiji era through to the first half of the twentieth century. Chapter 6 investigates how ideas about agriculture developed and were articulated in public policy debates in the second half of the twentieth century through a content analysis of national newspaper editorials relating to the two framework-setting agricultural basic laws of 1961 and 1999. Chapter 7 offers an analysis of public opinion survey data to show the most significant ideas shaping policy preferences towards agriculture for voters and consumers in Japan, from the 1970s until the present day.

Finally, Chapter 8 considers those most influential ideas in the context of recent policy developments at a time of severe structural problems in the agricultural sector, including domestic reform proposals under the administration of Abe Shinzō[8] and the reorientation of Japan's trade policy posture towards mega-regional trade agreements. It also examines two unfolding crises facing agriculture—the COVID-19 pandemic and anthropogenic climate change—and considers how future policy should respond in light of voters' policy preferences. The book concludes by arguing that ideas about agriculture have been historically important in the political economy of Japan, and that such ideas, particularly those of a non-economic nature, deserve greater scholarly and political attention.

1.4 The Methods

Three methods are employed in this study. First, to understand the historical and cultural origins of agrarian ideas an analytical survey of texts is undertaken, explicating important ideas and examining how consequential agrarian thinkers viewed agriculture and its role in the economy and society. Chapter 5 surveys a range of philosophers, policy-makers, and popular thinkers and their most important contributions to agrarian thought, from the early modern and modern era through to the first half of the twentieth century. These ideas are then classified in an original typology that charts the development of ideas about agriculture across this period.

Second, to understand the articulation and development of ideas over time, a content analysis of newspaper editorial articles is used to examine how farming was portrayed in public policy debates relating to the Agricultural Basic Law (*Nōgyō Kihon Hō*) of 1961, and the Food, Agriculture, and Rural Areas Basic Law (*Shokuryō Nōgyō Nōson Kihon Hō*) of 1999. The articles about these two laws, often called the "constitution(s) for agriculture" (*nōgyō no kempō*), were published in four major national newspapers, the *Yomiuri Shimbun*, the *Asahi Shimbun*, the *Mainichi Shimbun*, and the *Nikkei Shimbun*. The contents of these editorials are analysed in Chapter 6 to identify the ways in which newspapers framed the issues in question, the types of ideas being articulated, and how portrayals of agriculture compared across the two periods.

Third, to examine the predominant ideas among voters and consumers in contemporary Japan, Chapter 7 analyses historical and original public opinion survey data, from two sources. First, Cabinet Office surveys relating to attitudes towards agriculture and food are analysed to show longitudinal trends in popular sentiment since the 1970s. Then, to investigate more deeply the values and preferences shaping contemporary public opinion towards agriculture, the results of an original online survey are presented and analysed.

******

The content of this study will be of interest to a range of scholars in the social sciences and humanities, graduate and upper undergraduate students in various fields, and policy and business professionals working in the international trade sphere, as well as to the general reader with an interest in Japan. Scholars of economics, political economy, and political science (including those focusing on Japan, East Asia, comparative politics, and the role of ideas) will find in it both a clear theoretical framework and a long arc of supporting evidence in favour of the argument being advanced. Graduate and undergraduate students can engage with an innovative approach to Japan's political economy, as well as useful information from some lesser-trodden paths in Japan Studies. Policy and business professionals may obtain a better understanding of what is important to a majority of Japanese in discussions of agriculture and trade, and why, knowledge that would be of value when undertaking negotiations. And the general reader may also find interest in the discussions of historical ideas about agricultural as the foundation of Japanese society, and in seeing how those ideas originated and developed across decades and centuries.

All readers will hopefully find something else, too, in an era of backlash against the trends of globalisation and seemingly boundless marketisation that have characterised recent decades—the articulation of alternative views of the world, with deep historical roots in values relating to society and culture and human welfare. These views can serve as a useful means for contextualising dominant contemporary theories that focus heavily on economic welfare and material interests, often with insufficient attention to the many and complex ideas that we all have, and have always had, about human and societal flourishing and our collective wellbeing as one small part of a vast, interconnected natural world.

CHAPTER 2

THE POLITICAL ECONOMY OF JAPANESE AGRICULTURE: A BALANCE SHEET

The primary contention of this study is that the inclusion of ideational factors provides for a more complete account of the political economy of Japanese agriculture than approaches that focus only on material, institutional or political interests. This chapter surveys those interests in detail, to consider who gains and who loses, and whether these factors alone can sufficiently explain why an enduring majority of voters and consumers support Japan's protectionist agricultural policy regime. It does so by examining the economic and political costs and benefits of policy regime, including direct, indirect, and opportunity costs, as well as direct and indirect benefits. Where possible, empirical data or numerical estimates are given, and where such statistics are not available, the costs and benefits are detailed and analysed. Finally, a 'balance sheet' is provided to summarise these economic and political costs and benefits.

The economic costs of agricultural protection can be considered in a number of ways. One is the cost imposed on taxpayers who fund government expenditure on agricultural subsidies and other supports. A second is the costs imposed on consumers, considered in terms of food prices and tariffs, the Engel's coefficient, and consumers' share of the financial burden of support. Third, there are indirect economic costs, such as from using inefficient policy tools and in terms of societal health impacts. Fourth, there are the opportunity costs of forgone trade that result from pursuing protectionist agricultural trade policies. Finally, certain other kinds of market-distorting economic costs can also be identified.

In terms of economic benefits, trade theory shows that there are (usually) no net welfare benefits to a country from protectionist policies compared with free trade alternatives, but in addition to tariff revenues for the government, the current policy regime does improve the welfare of certain sectoral groups. In the case of Japanese agriculture, beneficiaries include farmers, the agricultural cooperative and interest group JA, and agriculture ministry bureaucrats. Advocates also contend that farmers provide substantial positive economic externalities in the form of environmental benefits.

The current policy regime would be expected a priori to produce a number of political costs. On the domestic level, agricultural protection affects the interests of the powerful business lobby, whose members' interests in global free trade clash with the agricultural sector's demands. It also reduces the material welfare of urban voters, who now account for over 90% of the electorate. On the international level, Japan's protectionist stance has been a cause of friction and disputes with major partners for much of the postwar era, most recently in Japan's bilateral and mega regional trade negotiations.

Conversely, political benefits also accrue from the provision of protection, both to individual politicians who build careers as representatives of rural areas, and for parties who gain from JA's ability to mobilise rural voters. Considered more broadly, agricultural protection also offers a functional equivalent to social and welfare policies that help stabilise rural incomes and make economically marginal communities more viable.

2.1 Economic Costs

Costs to taxpayers

Taxpayer subsidies to farmers are provided primarily through the Ministry of Agriculture, Forestry, and Fisheries (MAFF). The MAFF's regular budget in 2020 was 2.31 trillion yen.[9] Administrative costs were 677 billion yen, and a small share of the budget went to the forestry and fisheries sectors, implying that the amount of taxpayer money spent in support of farmers from the regular budget was in the region of 1.6 trillion yen.

In addition to the regular budget, the MAFF also frequently receives supplementary budgets, which cover expenditure such as 'countermeasures' (*taisaku*) to address the domestic impact of agricultural trade liberalisation. In the 2019 supplementary budget, the MAFF received 503 billion yen[10] to fund countermeasures subsequent to the Comprehensive and Progressive agreement for Trans Pacific Partnership (CPTPP), and in 2020 the figure was 545 billion yen.[11] According to Kazuhito Yamashita, the package of measures introduced to mitigate CPTPP-related beef import liberalisation alone will total around 3 trillion yen.[12]

Similar countermeasures were funded by the government in the late 1990s, ostensibly to offset the effects of the agricultural trade concessions made at the 1994 Uruguay Round of the GATT/WTO. However, much of this spending went not to farmers but rather on 'public works' construction projects in rural areas, and other tangential projects that did little to improve the structure or productivity of the farming sector. The total cost of the measures was around 6.01 trillion yen, or 55 billion U.S. dollars.[13]

Another way to consider the direct costs of agricultural support to taxpayers is by using the OECD's Producer Support Estimate (PSE). The PSE is defined as the "annual monetary value of gross transfers from consumers and taxpayers, arising from policies that support agriculture, regardless of their nature, objective or impacts on farm production of income" (OECD, 2009: 33). Percentage PSE is PSE calculated as a share of gross farm receipts including supports.

FIG 2-1: OECD PRODUCER SUPPORT ESTIMATES (%), 1986-2018

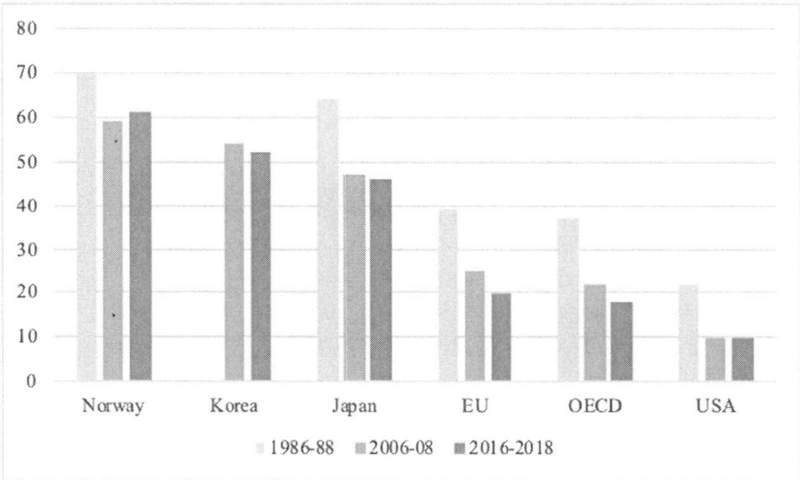

In percentage PSE terms, the data shows that Japan is an outlier among economically advanced countries. As seen in Figure 2-1, Japan's percentage PSE figure in the period 2016-18 averaged 46%, down from 64% in 1986-88 but largely unchanged since 2006-08. The value for Japan is more than double the averages for both the OECD (18%) and the EU (20%), while the equivalent figure for the United States is 10%, and for Australia 2%.

Overall, Japan recorded the third highest percentage PSE level in the OECD (OECD, 2013, 67), after Norway and Korea. In nominal terms, the OECD estimated that the value of producer support in Japan was 41.8 billion U.S. dollars in 2018, down from a peak of 62.5 billion dollars in 2012. The average value of support in the ten-year period to 2017 was 53.7 billion dollars (about 5.8 trillion yen) per year.

Costs to consumers

A second major economic cost is the cost to consumers. Trade theory indicates that imposing a tariff on imports reduces consumer surplus while increasing producer surplus. Consumers in Japan are forced to pay higher prices than under more a liberal trade regime, and also pay higher prices than peers in other economically advanced countries. In 1997, an Australian government report calculated that agricultural support was costing Japan over 70 billion dollars annually, with Japanese consumers paying around double the average world food prices (East Asia Analytical Unit, 1997, Chapter 9), a figure that is in line with OECD PSE estimations.

Comparing food price levels between countries is not a simple undertaking. One reason is differences in consumption patterns. As Flath (2000, 13) notes, representative consumption bundles differ between Japan and other countries at similar development levels, due to different revealed preferences. For example, a direct comparison of the prices of milk, bread, rice, beef, or tomatoes between Japan and other countries would be inexact, since relative demand for such items varies due to different culinary cultures and preferences. Exchange rate fluctuations also complicate comparisons of food price. Given these limitations, some of the better ways to examine the relative cost of food in countries are food tariff rates, the Engel's coefficient and Consumer Support Estimates.

Food tariff rates

In general, levels of protection in Japan vary considerably by commodity. Overall, the simple average of tariffs on agricultural products entering Japan was 23.3% in 2011, which was almost ten times the simple average tariff on industrial products of 2.5% in 2010 (Urata, 2015, 62-3). In international comparison, Japan's average agricultural tariff level exceeded the levels of the United States (5.0%) and the EU (13.9%), but was below those of Norway (55.8%), Korea (48.6%), and Switzerland (48.6%).

A straightforward way to see the specific costs of agricultural trade protection is to examine import tariffs on individual food items. Table 2-1 shows tariff levels for some common items in 2015 and 2020, that is, before and after the signing of the TPP/CPTPP agreement in which Japan made its most significant concessions to date on food tariffs. The table includes both the highest applied rates (general or WTO tariff rates) and the most preferential rates as applied to CPTPP countries.

The table demonstrates where the focus of protection is within the food tariff schedule. Soybeans and corn are among the many products that have no tariff. Lower-tariff items include most fruit such as cabbages, carrots, strawberries, pineapples, and oranges, rates on the last of which increase when Japanese *mikan* are in season. Poultry is also a lower-tariff item, while higher tariffs are found on dairy products, beef and pork, and rice.

TABLE 2-1: TARIFF SCHEDULES FOR SELECTED FOOD IMPORTS

Item	**2015**	**2020**	**2020 CPTPP**
Soybeans	0%	0%	0%
Corn (maize)	0%	0%	0%
Cabbages, carrots	5%	5%	0%
Shiitake mushrooms	12.8%	5%	3.6%
Strawberries (fresh)	6%	6%	0%
Oranges	16 to 32%	16 to 32%	8 to 25.6%
Pineapples (fresh)	23.8%	17%	12.4%
Milk	25%	25%	16.2%
Butter, cheese	35%	25%	16.2%
Poultry	14%	14%	5.9%
Beef	38.5%	38.5%	25.8%
Sugar	35 to 103 yen/kg	35 to 103 yen/kg	21.5 to 30.5 yen/kg after quota
Pork	361 yen/kg	361 yen/kg	93 to 393 yen/kg
Durum wheat	9.8 yen/kg	65 yen/kg	Free in quota
Rice	402 yen/kg	402 yen/kg	Free in quota

Source: Japan Customs

Items with the highest tariff liabilities are often assigned specific tariffs,[14] such as sugar, pork, durum wheat, and rice. While ad valorem equivalents of specific tariffs vary constantly with market price and currency fluctuations, these figures can reach extremely high levels for many products. For example, Harada calculated that ad valorem equivalents in 2013 were 218% for powdered milk, 234% for potato starch, 252% for wheat, 328% for sugar, 583% for tapioca starch, 778% for rice, and 1700% for the gelatinous root vegetable *konjac*.[15] Overall, the table shows that high levels of agricultural protection exist on certain major food items, benefitting the domestic farmers who produce those items, at the cost of higher prices for all Japanese consumers who purchase rice, meat, dairy produce, and other core food items.

The Engel's coefficient

An alternative method of comparing food costs is to examine aggregate household food expenditure across countries using the concepts of the 'Engel's coefficient' and 'Engel's Law'. The Engel's coefficient gives the percentage of average household income spent on food. Since income elasticity for food is less than one, at the national level Engel's Law predicts that the higher a country's per capita income, the lower the proportion of spending on food. The coefficient in countries with low per capita incomes is expected to be relatively high and in countries with high per capita incomes relatively low.

In the early Meiji period, the Engel's coefficient in Japan was estimated at over 60% (Hayami, 1988, 19). Figure 2-2 gives historical data for the Engel's co-efficient since 1935. Following an initial spike representing the period of severe food shortages after 1945, the data follow a long-term downward trend, in line with expectations for a growing economy with rising incomes. The figure was 36.4% in 1935 (prior to wartime disruption), 38.8% in 1960, and 30.4% in 1973. By the mid-1980s, it had declined to 27.0% and remained stable at around 23% from 1995 until 2010. However, in the most recent decade the trend line has turned upward, indicating that Japanese households have been spending an increasing percentage of total income on food. According to the national Statistics Bureau, households spent 25.7% of income on food in 2018.

Variations in statistical methodology can make international comparisons of Engel's coefficients difficult. For example, World Bank data for 2011 suggests that Japan's Engel's coefficient is 12.4% income, compared to

6.9% in the United States, 8.5% in the U.K., 10.2% in Germany, and 12.7% in Italy (Clement and Si, 2018). While these figures are lower than national government estimates, they confirm that Japan has one of the highest relative food costs among advanced economies, with Japanese spending almost double the share of income on food as U.S. consumers even by this lower estimate.

FIG. 2-2: ENGEL'S COEFFICIENT SINCE THE 1930S

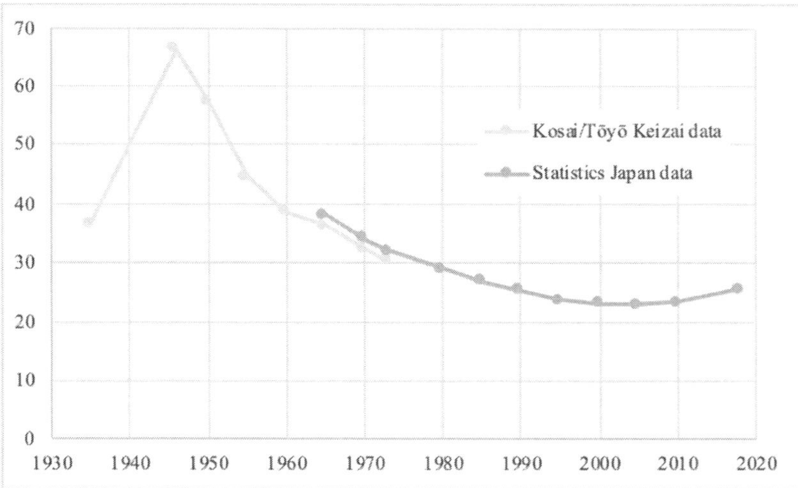

Source: Hayami (1988), Statistics Bureau of Japan (2019).

Consumer Support Estimates

A third method of measuring the cost to consumers is to use another OECD statistic, the Consumer Support Estimate (CSE). The CSE is defined as "an indicator of the annual monetary value of gross transfers to (or from) consumers of agricultural commodities, measured at farm gate level, arising from policy measures which support agriculture, regardless of their nature, objectives or impacts on consumption of farm products" (OECD, 2010). Negative CSE values indicate that consumers are net providers of support to producers, while positive figures mean that consumers are net beneficiaries.

Figure 2-3 demonstrates that Japanese consumers have borne a large financial burden every year for over 30 years, exceeding even that of consumers in the entirety of the European Union. In this period, the average annual transfer from Japan's consumers to agricultural producers in U.S. dollar terms was 58.7 billion, which exceeded the 46.6 billion in the European Union, 20.9 billion in South Korea, and 1.4 billion in Norway. In the United States, consumers received an effective subsidy of 14.1 billion.

The annual burden in Japan in U.S. dollar terms averaged 60.2 billion in the late 1980s, 70.4 billion in the 1990s, 50.3 billion in the 2000s, and 53.7 billion in 2010-2017. Notably, CSE levels in the European Union, which exceeded Japan's levels until 1992, decreased over time due to reforms to the Common Agricultural Policy, and averaged only half of Japan's levels in the most recent period, despite having a population more than three times larger.

FIG. 2-3: CONSUMER SUPPORT ESTIMATES, 1986-2017

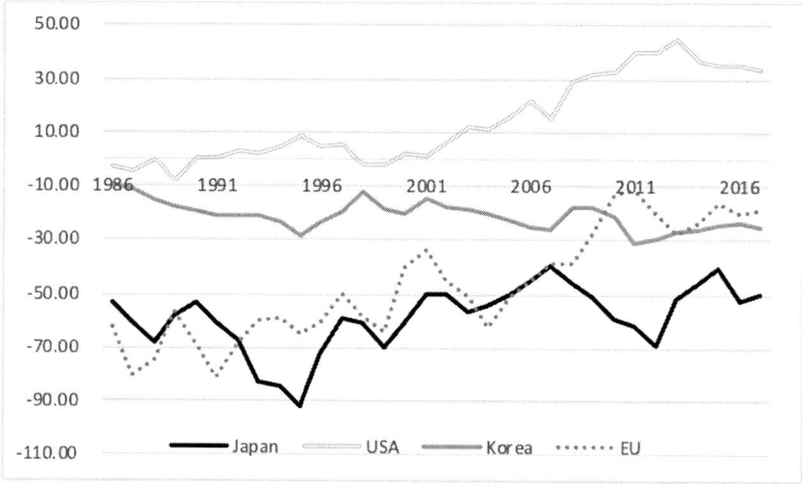

Source: OECD.

In addition to the direct costs to taxpayers and consumers detailed in the preceding pages, another important set of costs to consider are those that arise from the nature of the system that administers various supports and subsidies to agriculture. These costs are considered *indirect*, in that they arise not from the policy goals themselves but from the methods through which those policies are implemented. Indirect costs include political 'pork,' bureaucratic inefficiencies, and inefficient policy instruments.

Political pork

First, on the political side, there is the cost of farm-related *pork*. Pork (or 'pork barrel politics') refers to spending in geographically specific locations on public works and other government projects that may have little economic justification but which financially benefit preferred groups who in turn provide political support for the governing party or parties—in essence, a legal form of buying votes. Naturally, pork is never labelled as such on departmental budgets and its classification and estimation is necessarily a subjective undertaking, one person's pork being another person's essential public spending to boost an ailing local economy. Instead, likely instances may be given.

Perhaps the most expensive example is the 6 trillion yen spending package allocated in the 1990s for income support and rural construction projects agreed by the government as a form of compensation to farming and rural areas following the Uruguay Round Agreement on Agriculture reforms. Likewise, the 3 trillion yen package of countermeasures for the beef industry subsequent to CPTPP liberalisation measures is another prime example in this category.

Another possible porcine payment relates to Local Allocation Grants (*chihō kōfukin*), which are non-specified income transfers from central to local government. Using population density as a proxy for urban and rural status, Katz (2014) argues that rather than being a means of income transfer to relatively poorer prefectures, grants from the central government have gone disproportionately to rural prefectures regardless of their income level, and that rural prefectures hosting thirty-one single-member 'swing' seats, whose outcomes have influenced recent general elections, receive more than prefectures of comparable income levels that are not swing districts. As with the Uruguay Round and CPTPP countermeasures, some degree of pork seems likely, but disaggregating the political effect from calculations of genuine need in rural prefectures at a time of depopulation and resultant social and economic decline is challenging.

From one perspective these are costly pay-offs to farmers and the farm lobby for acquiescing to agricultural trade liberalisation measures. On the other hand, economists might consider such transactions a natural part of the trade-off that goes with Pareto-optimal trade liberalisation measures, namely that winners compensate losers to the extent of their losses, with the remainder representing the gains from trade to society as a whole. The relevant figure would then be the *net* gain from trade liberalisation after such transfers are made, rather than the gross figure.

Bureaucratic inefficiencies

A second set of indirect costs are those associated with the agricultural ministry bureaucrats in relation to the issues of *amakudari* and *gaikaku dantai*. 'Amakudari' means literally 'descent from heaven,' and refers figuratively to lucrative post-retirement jobs semi-governmental affiliated agencies created by the ministry itself to help administer the agricultural sector, termed *gaikaku dantai*, or in private companies that benefit from government spending in rural areas (Mulgan, 2005, 25).[16] One study found that of ninety-nine senior MAFF bureaucrats who retired during one twelve-month period, sixty-one moved on to placements in amakudari positions (Nakano, 2009). A Prime Minister's Office survey in 2000 found that two hundred former bureaucrats across various departments had received retirement allowances in excess of 30 million yen from the publicly-funded organisations in which they served after leaving their ministries (Mulgan, 2005, 32).

In past decades, the economic cost of this system also included inefficiency costs arising from possible non-competitive bidding processes in public works contracts and costs arising from alleged collusion by amakudari in regulatory bodies, although such activities are no longer legal. Of course, well-connected former senior bureaucrats securing prominent jobs in the sector they helped regulate is common in many countries, and overall the problem may be no worse in Japan than elsewhere.

Instrumental inefficiencies

The instruments used to administer policies can result in another set of economic costs. Trade theory holds that subsidies are always a more efficient means of protection since tariffs produce greater welfare losses, including the 'deadweight losses' of trade that does not take place because of higher prices. The logic is that, for domestic sectors that lose from international trade owing to a lack of comparative advantage, a lump-sum subsidy that is decoupled from output or price levels offers a means to compensate losers by exactly the amount that would be lost compared to a protectionist scenario, whereas tariffs and other means of protection cannot be targeted so precisely to compensate losers. As such, lower levels of decoupling represent inefficient income transfer systems, while higher levels indicate more efficient systems.

Historically, Japan has had one of the lowest levels of decoupling among economically advanced countries, at 0.7% in 1986-88, 1.9% in 1997-99, and then 12.5% in 2008-10 (OECD, 2013, 28). Even this higher rate remains far below recent levels in other advanced economies, such as the United States (58.6%) and the European Union (68.8%).

Rather than by lump-sum subsidies, the Japanese government delivers support through a range of less-efficient measures, including tariffs, import quotas (including simultaneous buy-and-sell programmes), and production quotas. A study by Sakuyama (2010) found evidence for two factors in explaining why the Japanese government chose to rely so much on tariffs. One was the 'revenue motive,' namely that tariffs provide a lower-cost way for the government to provide support, which is important since high levels of national debt create budgetary constraints for the government. The other derived from 'optimal obfuscation theory,' meaning that tax-payers typically understate the costs of tariffs while overstating those of subsidies.

In 2010, the new Democratic Party of Japan government proposed an 'individual household income support' system of direct payments to some rice farmers who met certain production targets and limits, subsequently extending the proposal to wheat and soybean producers (Mulgan, 2014: 594). Yet after 2012, the LDP administration of Abe Shinzō moved to rescind this efficiency-improving move and instead restructure the gentan scheme to encourage farmers to produce rice for feed and flour (Yamashita, 2015, 89-90), despite the replacement system being significantly more expensive (Honma, 2015, 115).

In addition to the reasons given by Sakuyama, two other factors may be important in explaining this costly choice of inefficient policy instruments. One is the relative stability of the tariff-based measures from year, and agricultural tribe politicians have suggested that a shift to budget-financed support would leave farmers exposed to annual Diet disputations over expenditure levels.[17] The other is the ways in which the tariff-based system benefits the business model of JA.

The former senior MAFF bureaucrat Kazuhito Yamashita has argued that high tariffs are essential to maintaining the current system on which JA's business model depends. Since it profits first from commission from sales of inputs like fertiliser and machinery and then again from related financial services via its banking arm *Norinchūkin*, JA has a strong institutional interest in maintaining high rice prices that allow the greatest number of economically marginal small-scale farmers to remain viable (Yamashita, 2015, 88). Prior to the conclusion of the TPP/CPTPP, JA's share of total sales for individual agricultural products was 67% for milk, 57% for vegetables, 48% for beef, 44% for rice, 39% for fruit, 23% for pork, 20% for chicken, and 16% for eggs (Honma, 2015, 113).

Health costs

A fourth set of indirect costs relate to public health. In simple terms, the cost of food may also create a negative externality with regard to the nation's health, since the high cost of fruit and vegetables appears to be leading to a decline in their consumption. According to a 2011 survey on health and nourishment by the Ministry of Health, Labor, and Welfare, consumers were eating 17% less fruit, 6% fewer vegetables and 24% less seafood in 2011 than a decade before.[18] Among respondents, 30% cited high costs as a major factor in influencing their choices. The survey also found that households with an annual income of less than 2 million yen ate fewer vegetables than average.

In reporting the findings, the health ministry stressed the importance of eating a balanced diet and noted that eating insufficient fruit and vegetables could raise the risk of certain illnesses. In essence, agricultural protection and consequent high food prices together act as a regressive tax on the poorest members of society and may reduce their long-term health and wellbeing. This point is often overlooked in ongoing debates about the regressive impacts of raising Japan's consumption tax. And while affected individuals will bear both health and financial costs most directly, taxpayers will also pay 70% or more of the medical treatment costs under Japan's co-payment health system.

Economic opportunity costs

A fourth area of costs are the opportunity costs implicit in pursuing agricultural protection. Since the 1980s, international trade economists have modelled the effects of liberalising Japan's economy including the agricultural sector using computable general equilibrium (CGE) models. The basic logic of these models is that liberalisation leads to a more efficient use of resources within and between countries, which over time boosts economic growth and international trade.[19]

The results of these studies indicate both the opportunity costs of the current policy regime and the effects of liberalisation on individual sectors and overall GDP. On the whole, these studies find that shrinkage would occur in the agricultural sector but that the Japanese economy as a whole would see an increase in economic welfare. In the political sphere, these results have been used as supporting evidence by both advocates of agricultural trade policy liberalisation, who cite net welfare gains, and by opponents of liberalisation, who emphasise the effects of structural change on farmers and others.

The results obtained by using these models can vary with the assumptions made in constructing them and the quality of the data (in terms of methods used to in collection, aggregation, and adjustment), and models are also sensitive to the parameter values that are used (Piermartini and Teh, 2005). As such, these studies are best used as broad indicators of the likely direction and magnitude of change, rather than as precise forecasts. On the other hand, the fact that foreign direct investment is exogenous in these CGE models (due to the complexity of modelling FDI effects) mean that it is possible that actual welfare gains may be even higher (Urata, 2007, 79). The findings of a selection of these papers are summarised in Table 2-2, including Japan-specific studies and regional-level studies that also relate to Japan. It is seen that all studies predict positive welfare gains for Japan, ranging from 0.3% of GDP to 2.5% or more. Since these gains are relative to a baseline of no liberalisation, they represent significant ongoing gains in economic welfare that compound over time, rather than one-off benefits.

Other market distortion costs

In addition to the costs to taxpayers and consumers, indirect costs, and trade-related opportunity costs, a number of costs arising from market distortions can be identified, both domestically and globally. First, there is the opportunity cost imposed on full-time, business-oriented farmers. As noted, in the current system JA maintains a dominant role in the supply of inputs, distribution and sales of outputs, and related financial services for the entire agricultural sector. Exempt from antimonopoly laws, JA's position distorts the markets for farm inputs, farm product sales, and agricultural finance. The costs of these market distortions, though difficult to estimate, are not insignificant.

TABLE 2-2: SELECT CGE ESTIMATIONS OF THE ECONOMIC EFFECTS OF AGRICULTURAL LIBERALISATION

Author(s)	Year	Major findings	Notes
Anderson and Tyers	1987	Cost of agricultural protection is equivalent to 1.2% of GDP per annum	Japan's policies also reduced world market prices and farming income globally
Roningen and Dixit	1991	Deadweight losses: each $1 of protection cost consumers $1.50	Rural households have 30% higher incomes than urban
Ichioka and Tachibanaki	1989	Lowering agricultural subsidies would lead to higher production levels in other industries	
Fujiki	2000	Import liberalisation could raise consumer welfare by 0.3% of GDP equivalent	Rice price would reduce by half
Bull and Roberts	2001	50% cut in protection would increase Japan's GDP 0.14%	World GDP would also increase by 0.14%
Brown et al	2003	2% increase in Japan's GDP from 33% cut in all tariffs	6% GDP gain from global free trade
Lee and van der Mensbrugghe	2007	GDP gains of 0.7% from ASEAN+3 liberalization, 1.2% from global free trade	Japan's agricultural sector would see significant shrinkage
Kawai and Wignaraja	2008	1.6% GDP gain from ASEAN+6 liberalization	
Petri et al	2011	1.2 to 1.4% GDP gains from Asian regional or TPP liberalisation	
Lee and Itakura	2014	1.2% GDP gains from RCEP, up to 2.0% from TPP	Improving agricultural productivity would boost gains
Petri and Plummer	2016	0.9% GDP increase by 2020, 2.5% higher by 2030	

Second is the cost of domestic investment diversion. Agricultural protection makes otherwise inefficient agricultural businesses viable. Economic theory holds that capital invested in agriculture could have been more productively invested in more efficient sectors of the economy, and the fact that it was not represents an ongoing opportunity cost.

Finally, as Anderson and Tyers (1987) noted, Japan's agricultural protection results in a distortion of world food markets. As one of the largest global food importers, Japan's agricultural trade policies have the ability to distort the world markets for rice and other agricultural products, including for lower income countries with internationally competitive agricultural sectors.

2.2 Economic Benefits

On the opposite side of the ledger are the economic benefits that may arise from the current agricultural policy regime. In practice, these are more difficult to enumerate than the corresponding costs. Tariff revenues accruing to the government from imports could be classified as an economic benefit to government finances, although in reality tariff costs are borne by consumers via higher prices, and can only be considered partial benefits. Tariffs revenues from agriculture, forestry, and fisheries imports amounted to 37.8 billion yen in 2011.[20] Similar partial economic benefits accrue to sectional interest groups, in particular to farmers, Japan Agriculture (JA), and bureaucrats, while there may also be positive externalities for the environment.

Farmers

The first set of beneficiaries in economic terms are farmers themselves. The OECD's Producer Support Estimates detailed earlier in the chapter suggest that in 2016-18 around 46% of Japanese farmers' incomes derived from government support and protection. In 2017, the average net income from agriculture for a full-time farmer was 1.91 million yen.[21] The PSE calculations imply that 884,000 yen of that income came from government support.

However, such averages disguise significant regional variations. In Hokkaido, the northernmost island of Japan and the region with the largest average farm size, average net income was 11.2 million yen, while in the Chūgoku region of central Honshū, the figure was 712,000 yen. Furthermore, of the

1.33 million commercially operating farm households in 2015, only 22% were classified as 'business farms' by the agriculture ministry, while 19% were 'semi-business' and 59% were 'side-business' farms.[22] It follows that the economic benefits of agricultural protection accrue in large part to about 800,000 farming households with very small scale operations, for whom farming is a side-job or hobby-type interest, and who would struggle to be commercially viable without such support.

Japan Agriculture

A second economic beneficiary of the current policy regime is Japan Agriculture (JA), known as *Nōkyō* (meaning 'agricultural cooperative') in Japanese. A member-based cooperative, JA has its origins in two prewar antecedents, *Sangyō Kumiai* ('Industrial Cooperatives') and *Nōkai* ('Agricultural Society'), the latter of which was transformed into the *Teikoku Nōkai* ('Imperial Agricultural Society') in the 1930s (Freiner, 2019). In the postwar period Nōkyō became a cornerstone of the agricultural policy system, with semi-state functions in distribution and the administration of government policies (Bullock, 1997). It also developed extensive political power due to its ability to mobilise the rural electorate and influence politicians and policy.

Today, JA has a complex organisational structure consisting of local-level cooperatives, prefectural-level bodies, and eight national peak organisations, including JA-Zenchū (the Central Union of Agricultural Co-operatives), Zennoh (the National Federation of Agricultural Co-operative Associations), Zenkyōren (or JA-Kyōsairen, the National Mutual Insurance Federation of Agricultural Cooperatives), and the Norinchūkin bank.[23] This structure gives it presence in practically every town and village in Japan, a level of coverage unmatched by any private corporation or civil society institution in the nation. Today, the business operations of JA cover areas as diverse as trading, marketing, inputs, food processing, distribution, supermarket retailing, oil, health care, funeral services, real estate, cultural centres, agricultural colleges, newspaper publishing, a travel agency, and banking and finance (see Mulgan, 2011; JA-Zenchū, 2020).

In 2019, JA had 627 cooperatives and a total membership of 10.49 million, of which 4.25 million were regular (i.e. farmer) members and 6.24 million were associate (i.e. non-farmer) members.[24] From these members, JA's banking arm held deposits of 10.47 trillion yen.[25] Norinchūkin's banking business is about as large as that of the leading mega-bank Mitsui

Sumitomo, and Zenkyōren's insurance business is almost as large as Nippon Life Insurance Company, Japan's second largest insurance firm (Honma, 2015, 107). Overall, gross profits from JA's diverse business portfolio were around 1.8 trillion yen in fiscal 2018.[26]

While financial activities make up a significant share of business operations and profits (Yamashita, 2014, 32), agriculture remains the backbone of JA's activities and identify. Through its various divisions, JA can loan money to farmers at below-market rates for the purchase of inputs and farm machinery (Freiner, 2019, 81), arrange the distribution and sale of farm produce, then have farmers deposit the earnings into Norinchūkin accounts. With its dominant position in farming services markets, JA has a strong institutional interest in maintaining the current policy regime and maximising the number of small-scale, part-time farmers as captive customers.

Finally, peak JA also profits from its regulatory and administrative functions for local cooperatives. For example, the levies collected by JA-Zenchū for providing auditing and other services to local cooperatives amounted to around 8 billion yen, and provide a significant source of income to its political activities (Mulgan, 2016). Despite some movements towards reform in the postwar era by the Abe administration, detailed in Chapter 8, in financial terms JA remains the largest winner in the postwar agricultural policy regime.

Bureaucrats and others

In addition to the institutional benefits accruing to the ministry as a whole, on an individual level agricultural bureaucrats also benefit financially from the current policy regime. There are more than fifty MAFF-affiliated gaikaku dantai to which amakudari bureaucrats descend. These include such organisations as the National Association of Regional Horse Racing, the National Chamber of Agriculture, the Japan Agriculture, Forestry and Fisheries Promotion Association, and the Agricultural Policy Promotion Council (Mulgan, 2000, 510–11).

The funds allocated to these groups have been substantial. One study found that the MAFF in 1998 allocated 98 billion yen to fifty-six gaikaku dantai, including 52.8 billion yen to the 'Agriculture, Forestry and Fishery Groups Staff Members' Mutual Aid Association', and 17 billion yen to the National Land Improvement Fund Association (Mulgan, 2000, 118-121). From the perspective of senior bureaucrats, who are typically elite university graduates who work for decades in public sector jobs, these positions serve to boost total career earnings.

Finally, the construction sector has also benefitted from agricultural support. The tendency to channel countermeasure funding towards public works has resulted in spending on a range of construction projects in rural areas, such as road improvements, tunnels and bridges, reinforcing river banks with concrete, and building community centres. Major and minor construction firms, as well as many local subcontractors, have all benefitted from such projects.

Environmental benefits

Advocates of the current agricultural policy regime assert that the 'multifunctionality' (*tamenteki kinō*) of agriculture as a sector means that it brings significant economic benefits through positive externalities related to the environment and society. The issue of multifunctional agri-environmental issues was first addressed in policy in the 1992 New Policy for Food, Agriculture and Rural Areas, and includes such areas as the protection of water, soil and landscape resources, biodiversity, and food safety.

The most detailed calculations of the economic benefits of these functions have been made by JA-Zenchū. Using a "substitutive cost method" to impute the value of agricultural externalities in terms of land and environmental protection, JA economists calculated that the sector provides indirect economic benefits equivalent to 8.2 trillion yen per year (JA-Zenchū, 2020). As shown in Table 2-3, these figures include the following functions: flood prevention, recreational amenities, fostering water resources, preventing landslides, preventing soil erosion, recycling waste into fertilisers, and moderating summer heat.

These figures must be treated with a degree of caution for at least three reasons—they date from a 2005 study, the methodology and assumptions are unclear, and they are from an organisation with a political interest in demonstrating high values. Economic theory also holds that indirect means are always less efficient tools for delivering goals like flood prevention than direct measures, since they cannot be targeted so precisely.

TABLE 2-3: ESTIMATED ECONOMIC VALUES OF POSITIVE EXTERNALITIES OF JAPANESE AGRICULTURE

Positive externality	Annual estimate (¥)	Definition	Estimation method
Flood prevention	3500 bn	"Water storage capacity of paddy fields and upland fields" during rainy season	"Evaluated in the form of the function played by flood control dams in the country"
Recreational amenities	2400 bn	"Values of visits by urban people enjoying rural landscape and recreational amenities"	Estimated value of these visits
Fostering water resources	1500 bn	"Water storage capacity of paddy fields and upland fields" during rainy season	"Evaluated in the form of the function played by flood control dams in the country"
Preventing landslides	478.2 bn	"Average amount of damage in the estimated number of landslides prevented by cultivation of farmland"	Estimated value of this damage
Preventing soil erosion	331.8 bn	"Amount of soil erosion prevented by cultivation of farm lands"	"Evaluated in form of construction costs of dams for soil erosion prevention in the country"
Recycling waste into fertiliser	12.3 bn	"Amount of waste including food leftovers recycled into organic fertilisers"	"Evaluated in the form of the total cost of such waste treatment in the cities"
Moderating summer heat	8.7 bn	"The temperature lowering capacity of paddy fields in the summer season"	"Evaluated in the form of the air conditioner costs"
Total	8.2 trillion		

Source: JA-Zenchū (2020)

At the same time, the agricultural sector clearly *does* provide major positive externalities in relation to the functions described, embedded assumptions are to be found in all economic models (including trade models), and even academic economists are not immune to biases, as Chapter 3 demonstrates. As such, JA's figures could best be interpreted in the same manner as the CGE figures in the previous table—to indicate the relative direction and magnitude of benefits, rather than precise economic values.

2.3 Political Costs

For governments with finite budgets, privileging agricultural interests inevitably means less preferential treatment for other constituencies. Postwar governments in Japan were dominated by the hegemony of the Liberal Democratic Party (LDP) in the so-called '1955 Political System.' The LDP formed every government from 1955 until 1994, was returned to power in successive coalitions from 1995 until 2009, and has been in office in coalition again since 2012. While opposition to the provision of agricultural support and protection was initially muted during the first years of the 1955 system, over time the direct costs and opportunity costs grew, and advocates of reform latterly became increasingly vocal. The two political constituencies whose interests have been most negatively affected by agricultural protection are the business lobby and urban voters.

Business lobby

The most prominent example of a competing interest group in the agricultural policy sphere is the business lobby. The foremost national business organisation is *Keidanren* (also known in English as the 'Japan Business Federation'), whose 1400 members include almost all of Japan's major firms. Writing in the late 1980s, Kent Calder commented at that time that Keidanren had "declaimed bitterly about farm support programs for more than a generation" but had had "little success in forestalling rice support price increases until the early 1980s, despite the huge national budgetary deficits that began after the 1973 oil shock" (Calder, 1989, 231). More recently, Mulgan took the view that business organisations such as Keidanren, while occasionally facing accusations of "agricultural bashing," had not campaigned as forcefully or consistently for agricultural policy reform as might have been expected (Mulgan, 2014, 589).

Following Japan's international trade policy shift to pursue FTAs and Economic Partnership Agreements (EPAs) from around 2000, Keidanren played a prominent role in the negotiation processes. For example, it helped set the agenda for items to be included in Japan's first ever FTA with Singapore, it was reportedly the major player pushing forward the FTA with Mexico (which saw the partial liberalisation of pork and orange juice imports), and it played a central role in coordinating business interests in both countries during negotiations for the unsuccessful FTA talks with Korea (Yoshimatsu, 2005). Keidanren has also engaged in lobbying the MAFF and agriculture-focused politicians in an attempt to counter the influence of the agricultural lobby (Yoshimatsu, 2005, 271).

When the focus of trade policy shifted to mega-regional agreements in the 2010s, Keidanren strongly advocated Japan's participation in the proposed TPP, the Regional Comprehensive Economic Partnership (RCEP) involving 15 Asia-Pacific states, and the Japan-EU EPA. In 2013, Keidanren called for enhancing the competitiveness of the agricultural sector by allowing farm consolidation and scale expansion, and the implementation of a direct payment scheme as a means of facilitating the structural changes that these reforms would require.[27] It also outlined a roadmap to make agriculture a "Leading- Edge Growth Industry" by developing the "Food Value Chain" and boosting exports.[28] Given that Japan concluded fifteen bilaterals and five regional or mega-regional trade agreements between 2001 and 2020, the business lobby clearly has had some success in pursuing its political and economic agendas.

At the same time, the concessions sought and usually secured by the government for the agriculture sector in trade negotiations have imposed an opportunity cost on Japan's multinational corporations. The rapidly negotiated deal with the United States in 2019 distilled the typical pattern of these negotiations, with the Japanese government emphasising market access for its auto makers while seeking to avoid major concessions on its agricultural market.[29] This again demonstrated that agricultural support and protection in Japan comes at a political cost for the business lobby, although this cost has lessened in recent years as the government accepted incrementally greater agricultural trade liberalisation in agreements.

Urban voters

Rational choice political economy approaches predict that urban voters would oppose agricultural protection and vote against parties who offered it, since urban voters have their marterial welfare reduced by such policies. As seen in Figure 2-4, the share of urban residents in postwar Japan increased rapidly from 63% in 1960 to 75% in 1974, and then again from 79% in 2000 to 91% in 2010. As of 2018, 92% of Japanese residents lived in urban areas, and these citizens bore the main financial costs of protection and support policies for rural agricultural areas, both as taxpayers and as consumers.

In reality, an enduring majority of voters returned LDP governments in all but four years since 1955, and public opinion surveys since the 1970s showed consistently high support for policies that helped farmers and imposed financial costs on urban consumers, as detailed in Chapter 7. In addition, during the period in which rice prices were determined annually by the government (until the early 1990s), almost all opposition parties called for even higher price levels than the LDP provided, implying that agricultural protection had very broad appeal across the spectrum (Horiuchi and Saito, 2010, 429).

FIG. 2-4: URBAN SHARE OF THE POPULATION SINCE 1960

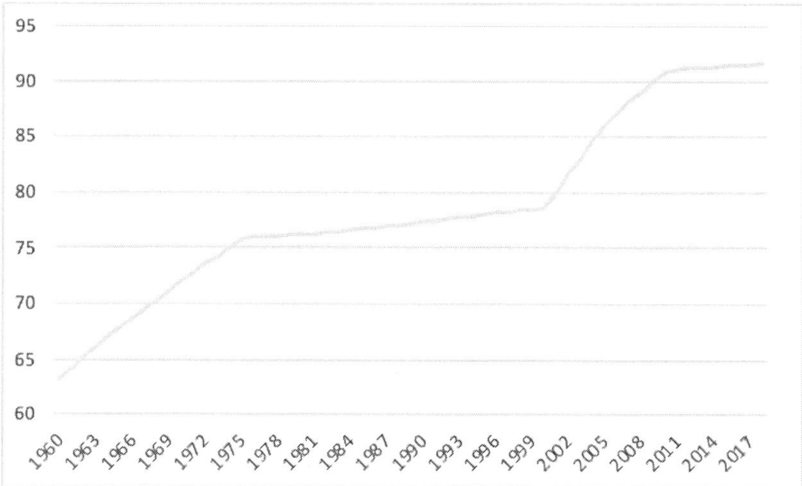

Source: World Bank (2020).

International political costs

Japan's protectionist agricultural policy regime has been called "one of the most notorious examples of trade protection in the world," and has "seriously degraded the reputation of Japanese trade policies" (Ando and

Kimura, 2008, 1-2). Since the 1950s, it has often been a source of tension with other countries, limiting the nation's economic policy options and causing trade frictions with even Japan's most important economic partners and political allies.

From the end of the Occupation until the early 1960s, Japanese governments seeking to rebuild the economy pursued a protectionist growth-oriented trade policy in all sectors (Flath, 2000, 155). According to Cortell and Davis (2005, 10), Japan's "embrace of mercantilism" during this early postwar period was "well-documented". Such discriminatory trade policies were largely indulged by the United States, Japan's main military ally and trading partner, for Cold War-related strategic political reasons. However, as early as 1955, the United States government exerted pressure on Japan to import more of its surplus agricultural products, resulting in a bilateral agreement in which Japan agreed to take U.S. food including rice (Calder, 1989, 263-4).

By the early 1960s, the Japanese economy had largely recovered from wartime disruption, and pressure for market access increased from the U.S. and other countries (Kosai, 1989, 522). The 1960 "Trade and Foreign Exchange Liberalisation Plan Outline" was a major step towards liberalising Japan's trade in agriculture and other areas, and paved the way for Japan to become a major agricultural importer (Honma, 2015, 108). The number of import-restricted agricultural items fell from 68 in 1963 to 23 in 1973 (Urata, 2015, 48-49). During the presidency of Richard Nixon (1969-74), Japan's agricultural protectionism became a greater problem in bilateral relations with the U.S., with restrictions on imports of beef and oranges creating new frictions (Itoh, 1994). In 1974-75, when the United States imposed an embargo on exports of soybeans in order to prioritise domestic animal feed, Japan was significantly affected as a major importer.

By the early 1980s, further agricultural trade liberalisation had again lowered Japan's food self-sufficiency rate (Honma, 2015, 109). Even so, disputes over agricultural trade restrictions intensified in the 1980s, with the United States, Australia, and New Zealand together lodging a complaint that Japan's restrictions were in breach of GATT Article XI:I (Dyck, 1998). An agreement to phase out quotas on beef and citrus fruits was finally reached in 1988. From 1986 until 1994, agricultural protection was a cause of intense international pressure for Japan during negotiations for the Uruguay Round of the GATT/WTO talks. The Japanese government ultimately agreed to the tariffication of non-tariff barriers in the Uruguay Round Agreement on

Agriculture. Rice was initially excluded but subsequently added when it became clear that the costs of exclusion were unsustainably high, in what Itoh (1994) termed the *kome kaikoku* ('opening the country to rice').[30] In the 1990s, agriculture was also a significant stumbling block in the APEC negotiations between Asia-Pacific governments, and Japan's refusal to agree to liberalisation in the fisheries and forestry sectors helped undermine the so-called 'Early Voluntary Sectoral Liberalization' initiative in 1997 (Ravenhill, 2001, 181, 184).

When Japan switched its focus from multilateral negotiations to a bilateral FTA-oriented trade strategy from around 2000 onwards, agricultural liberalisation remained a sensitive issue in discussions. Japan's trade agreements tended to be of a lower level or lower quality than those by other countries, mainly because of the exceptional treatment afforded to agricultural products (Urata, 2015, 61). Early agreements were pursued with countries who were not agricultural exporters, like Singapore, or developing countries to whom 'technical assistance' for agriculture was offered in lieu of agricultural liberalisation (Mulgan, 2015, 6).

The first agreement with an advanced agricultural exporting nation did not occur until the Japan-Australia EPA, launched in 2007 and signed in 2014. Throughout the negotiations, Australia sought full market access for sensitive items such as beef, wheat, dairy products, and sugar. When an agreement was finally reached to phase in lower tariffs for Australian beef and dairy exports, one interpretation was that both Australia and Japan were making strategic compromises ahead of the proposed TPP (Honma, 2015, 100).

Throughout this period, the Japanese government offered a range of justifications for protecting domestic agriculture. In 2003, Japan was one of 65 countries that restricted U.S. beef imports following the first reported case of bovine spongiform encephalopathy (BSE) there. In 2004, when the issue of 'sensitive products' was introduced at the Doha Round of WTO negotiations, Japan sought exemptions for various agricultural items including rice, wheat, barley, sugar, dairy products, beef, pork, and starch (Yamashita, 2015, 80-81). In 2012, Japan blocked imports of beef from Brazil following reports of BSE in a single cow there in 2010, even though those reports were disputed by the Brazilian government.[31] The readiness of the Japanese government to enact such restrictions raised suspicions that they were being used as cover for protecting domestic cattle farmers.

Agriculture remained an issue in trade negotiations into the 2010s. In the Japan-EU EPA negotiations from 2012 to 2018, the EU was concerned with high tariff barriers on beef, dairy products, and wine, tariff rate quotas on items such as pork, and a variety of non-tariff barriers such as approvals procedures for food additives and import restrictions on beef. Similarly, when Japan joined negotiations for the TPP in 2013, the government resolved to make certain categories of agricultural products off-limits in negotiations (Solis, 2017, 152). Termed *sei'iki*, meaning 'sacred' or 'sanctuary' items, and often listed as 'five' categories, the items were rice, wheat and barley, beef and pork, sugar and starch crops, and dairy products. In tariff classification terms, these products actually amounted to 586 separately classified items. The TPP Affairs Committee of the LDP said that the items should be protected as 'vital' or 'life or death' interests (*shikatsuteki rieki*), and that the government should withdraw from negotiations if exemptions were not achieved (Mulgan, 2015, 9).

Ultimately, the Japanese government did concede some agricultural liberalisation measures in its mega-regional agreements. In the TPP and CPTPP, Japan agreed to increased quotas for rice imports and the phased reduction of beef and pork tariffs, for example with the beef tariff falling from 38% to 9% over 20 years (see Table 2-1). Though the United States withdrew from the TPP in 2017, the 2019 US-Japan FTA put U.S. producers of wine, butter, milk, beef, and pork on the same tariff schedule as CPTPP participants. In the EU agreement, Japan removed tariffs on many cheeses and wines and increased import quotas for beef and pork, as well as agreeing to recognise EU geographical indicators.

2.4 Political Benefits

The basic reason why politicians provide financial support to any sectional interest group is to secure electoral benefits in return. In the case of Japanese agriculture, the benefits may be considered in two areas: to the LDP as a party, for whom rural areas represented a stable electoral base; and to individual rural politicians, whose election prospects are linked to the farming vote and the agricultural lobby.

Benefits to the LDP

In the late 1940s, as Japan's new political system was being established, rural support levels for the politically conservative Liberal Party stood around 25%, more than ten percentage points behind the national average

(Calder, 1989, 254). By the end of the 1950s, a period during which the government purchase price for rice more than doubled, rural support for the successor Liberal Democratic Party had risen to around 43%, almost ten percentage points higher than the national average. After 1960, the rural and national levels went on diverging trends, with rural support for conservatives rising from around 50% to well over 60% by 1980, and the national average declining from around 40% to 35%. Calder posits that rural voters were influenced by the government rice price increasing by more than 350% in the same period. Successive LDP governments clearly derived significant electoral benefits from providing agricultural protection during the postwar decades, using it to help establish and maintain a stable electoral base in rural Japan.[32]

However, securing the rural vote through agricultural support must be set against the context of rapid urban migration, as discussed above. Indirectly, these population movements had a political effect that served to amplify the voice of rural voters at the expense of urban residents. The reform of electoral districts did not keep pace with migration trends, with the result that rural districts became effectively over-represented in the Diet.[33] Legal cases regarding the constitutionality of these disparities have been pursued since 1962 and the Supreme Court has ruled that voter disparity in recent elections has been 'in a state of unconstitutionality,' stopping short of judging them 'unconstitutional'. Facilitated by this legal grey area, malapportionment increases the electoral benefits available to parties who offer agricultural support and protection as a means to attract voters.

Benefits to individual politicians

Agricultural protection also provides electoral benefits to individual politicians connected to rural constituencies or agricultural interests. While definitions can be loose and categories not mutually exclusive, these include *nōson gi'in* ('farm politicians' or rural Diet members), *nōrin gi'in* ('agriculture and forestry Diet members'), *Nōkyō gi'in* (Diet members who previously worked for JA), and, most significantly, *nōrin zoku* ('agricultural tribe politicians', or LDP Diet members active in agricultural policy circles). By one measure, the number of Diet members with some notable degree of connection to agricultural interests or agricultural policy was between 50% and 58% in every parliament between 1986 and 1998 (Mulgan, 2000, 480-483).[34]

In addition to channelling central government spending to rural districts, influential individual politicians have been able to help secure their own seats by obtaining protection for items whose production or cultivation is geographically concentrated in their own constituencies. Production geography can be a politically relevant factor if a product is dominant nationally or in a given region (Mulgan, 2000, 19). Examples of geographically concentrated products with high tariffs include include wheat (Hokkaidō, northern Kantō, northern Kyūshū), barley (northern Kantō, northern Kyūshū), milk and butter (Hokkaidō), peanuts (Chiba, Ibaraki), beef (Hokkaido, Tōhoku, southern Kyūshū) and konjac (Urata, 2015, 64-65). The highest ad valorem equivalent tariff of all, at up to 1700%, is on konjac, production of which is concentrated in Gunma prefecture. As Mulgan notes, the production center for is in Gunma, and between 1947 and 1993, Gunma's four-member District Number 3 was represented by four politicians who would subsequently serve as prime minister of Japan—Fukuda Takeo, Nakasone Yasuhiro, Obuchi Keizō, and Fukuda Yasuo.

Social policy benefits to rural communities

Agricultural support and protection also has benefits when considered in terms of its effects as social policy or welfare policy. While categorised and implemented separately from welfare spending, agricultural trade protection, subsidies to farming households, rural public works spending, and other policies can be functionally equivalent to welfare spending in terms of their effect and can help make economically marginal rural communities more viable. Here, two aspects are considered—the stabilisation effect on rural communities through income support, and as a supplementary pension for the elderly in rural communities.

Agricultural support policies undoubtedly served to help stabilise rural communities during periods of depopulation by supporting incomes. In the immediate postwar years, excess labour supply from overseas returnees was absorbed into the agricultural sector, resulting in 'work-sharing' and making the sector inefficient (Calder, 1989). During the rapid industrialisation of the 1950s and 1960s, surplus labour moved from farms to factories in a wave of urbanisation that benefitted the national economy as a whole but came at the cost of much social upheaval, including a growing rural-urban income gap by the late 1950s. The MAFF estimated that farm household income was 90% of non-farm household income in 1960 (OECD, 2009), though other estimates have put the figure as low as 68% (Estevez-Abe, 2008).

The 1961 Agricultural Basic Law mandated that future agricultural policy should aim to expand agriculture and raise productivity, stabilise prices to reduce inter-sectoral income disparities, increase farm size and farmer independence, promote farmer education programs, and improve farm welfare by improving rural living conditions (Calder, 1989, 266). Kent Calder has argued that the subsequent implementation of agricultural support turned agricultural spending into welfare policy by focusing on price support mechanisms without encouraging farm consolidation or economies of scale (1989, 267).

Similarly, Margarita Estevez-Abe has explained the provision of support policies for agricultural and rural communities in terms of functional equivalence. In essence, such policies as public works, subsidies to rural families, market-restricting regulations, and employment protections are used by governments to protect the livelihood of citizens. Utilising these tools allowed the Japanese government to target specific, electorally important groups such as farmers without having to raise taxes and without this spending being categorised as social welfare spending (Estevez-Abe 2008, 3, 4).

Today, as the farming population has aged more rapidly than the average worker, agricultural supports can also be considered as a kind of supplementary pension that help recipients remain resident in rural areas and contribute to community sustainability. According to the most recent MAFF data, the average farmer in 2015 was aged 66.1 years, up from 64.5 years in 2010.[35] As seen in Figure 2-5, almost half of all farmers are aged 70 or over, with only 23% aged under 60. Given this age profile, agricultural support policies benefit elderly farmers the most.

FIG. 2-5: SHARE OF FARMERS BY AGE CATEGORY

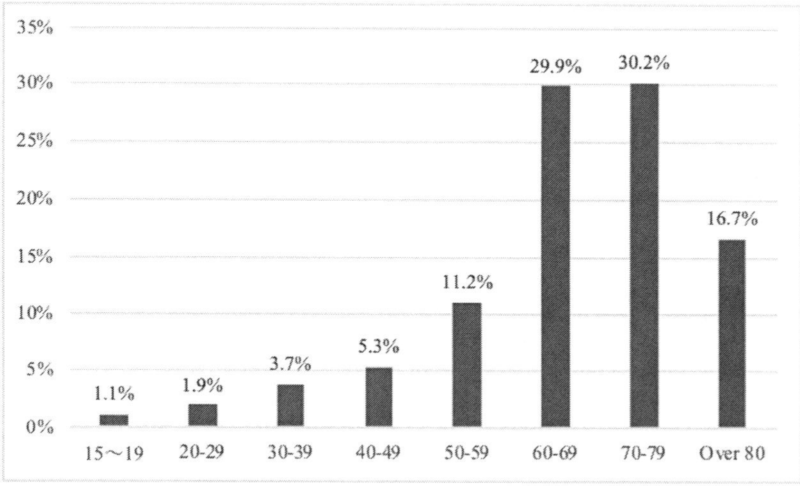

MAFF, *93rd Statistical Yearbook.*

2.5 A Political Economy Balance Sheet

The costs and benefits associated with agricultural policy are manifold and complex. This chapter has sought to categorise and estimate the major costs and benefits in both economic and political terms. The results are summarised in the political economy balance sheet presented in Table 2-4. While the nature of some costs and benefits make precise numerical estimations difficult, it is seen in the table that in economic terms, the costs are greater and more numerous than the benefits derived from agricultural protection. Conversely, with regard to political issues, the list of benefits is longer and more substantial than the costs.

Economically, the benefits accrue mainly to farming households and rural residents, and to JA and bureaucrats. Conversely the costs are borne by urban residents, who comprise 92% of the population, as both taxpayers and consumers. Business interests also suffer, in the context of international trade. Politically, there have been significant benefits to the LDP as a party and for individual politicians through the provision of protection, while the political costs have been relatively small domestically.

Returning to the question with which the chapter began, the data presented in the balance sheet fails to explain the paradox of urban voters, who bear the economic burden of agricultural support and protection as taxpayers and consumers yet remain supportive of the LDP and politicians who offer such policies. Indeed, as Chapter 7 will show, there is evidence of strong urban support for the current agricultural policy regime, not just indirectly in terms of electoral outcomes but directly for the specific policies themselves. Rational choice-based political economy approaches hold that as the number of farmers decrease and the number of non-farm workers increase, protectionism would start to decline, but a protectionist regime for agriculture has remained largely in place even as the urban population share has exceeded 90%.

Why should this be? One answer could be the *visibility* of costs and benefits. Many significant costs of the policy regime have low visibility. Tariffs hide the cost of protection that would be much clearer if the same support was given through direct payments to farmers; the amakudari system hides the true cost of employing senior civil servants; and agricultural supports hide the costs of providing extra income to rural communities and pensioners. It could be that voters and consumers are not conscious of the true scale of the costs of agricultural protection, and as such have imperfect information about their own economic welfare. The corollary of this information deficit argument is that popular support for agriculture could be reversed once accurate information becomes more widely known. For rational choice theories of agricultural policy, it also offers a potential auxiliary variable to explain the urban voter paradox.

However, for this argument to hold, two conditions must be met: (1) that voters and consumers have imperfect information about the true financial and economic costs of agricultural protection, and (2) that the policy preferences of voters and consumers are primarily determined by their material interests. Concerning the first point, while the costs may have been obscured in part, the prominent public debates about agricultural policy and related issues that have taken place over many years in relation to both domestic politics and international trade have undoubtedly given prominence to the overall costs of protection, including the multiplicity of costs listed above. Rational choice scholars who would advance this argument must prove that many voters and consumers have an erroneous understanding of their 'true' (material) interests; Neo-Marxists would term this a 'false consciousness' hypothesis.

TABLE 2-4: A POLITICAL ECONOMY BALANCE SHEET FOR JAPAN'S AGRICULTURAL POLICY REGIME

Issue/Group	Cost estimate	Issue/Group	Benefit estimate
	Economic		
MAFF budget	¥2.73 tn in 2020 ¥3 tn beef countermeasures after CPTPP	Farmers: Higher income	¥2.61 trillion in fiscal 2014; average farmer income of ¥1.22 million
Producer Support Estimate	¥5.76 tn per year on average, 2008-18	JA Group	¥1.8 trillion per year in group profits
Tariffs	Simple tariff average of 23.2% on food imports, much higher ad valorem equivalents on rice and other items	Tariff revenue	¥37.8 billion per year
Engel's coefficient	25.7% of household income spent on food in 2018	Positive externalities for the environment	Up to ¥8.2 trillion
Political 'pork'	¥6 tn Uruguay Round countermeasures, 1990s	Bureaucrats	End-of-career compensation for public sector salaries
Bureaucratic costs	Over ¥30 million in indirect funding per *amakudari* bureaucrat in second careers	*Gaikaku dantai*	Creation of jobs in regulatory and policy-related organisations

Inefficient policy tools	Deadweight losses, low levels of decoupling of support payments	Construction firms	Rural public works projects
Health costs	Lower consumption of fruit and vegetables due to high costs, particularly for low-income families		
Economic opportunity costs	Up to 2% GDP growth forgone annually due to protectionism		
Food market distortion	Negative impacts on domestic input prices, investment diversion, and overseas food producers		
	Political		
Competing demands from interest groups	Possible loss of some support from corporate sector or urban voters	LDP	Securing large and reliable electoral base in rural areas
International trade conflict	Restrictions on options in trade negotiations, and ill will from negotiating partners	Individual politicians	Securing financial, organisational and campaign support from JA Securing own seat by advancing general or specific protectionist policies
		Rural communities	Boosting rural incomes helped stabilise communities during periods of rapid urban migration

Concerning the second point, Japanese public opinion survey data since the 1970s strongly suggest that economic and price factors are relatively low priorities for voters in relation to agriculture and food policy. This data is presented and analysed in Chapter 7. If the policy preferences of voters and consumers *are* shaped at least in part by factors other than economic welfare concerns, as this study contends, it would be an entirely rational choice for individuals to support protectionist agricultural policies that reduced their own material welfare if such policies were instrumental for achieving other, more valued goals. To better understand these conflicting conceptions, Chapter 3 turns to the question of rationality in public policy analysis.

CHAPTER 3

RECONSIDERING RATIONALITY IN PUBLIC POLICY ANALYSIS

The structure of costs and benefits surveyed in Chapter 2 helps explain why *policymakers* may find it rational to continue the regime of agricultural support and protection for political reasons, despite high economic costs. However, the political economy balance sheet does not explain why *voters* consistently support policies that reduce their material welfare. To ask the question in the language of rational choice, why are voters behaving in such an *irrational* way? Or conversely, if we assume that voters do behave rationally, in what sense can voter attitudes towards Japan's agricultural policy regime be considered rational?

To answer this question, it is necessary to (re)consider the word *rational* in the context of public policy. This chapter explores the meaning and usage of rationality with regard to public policy-making and in the fields of economics and political science, and examines some of the fundamental philosophical assumptions that underpin rational choice-based analyses of the political economy of Japan. Turning to the possible goals, or maximands, that the current policy regime may achieve for voters, the chapter then considers some preliminary evidence about the sorts of ideas that are commonly expressed in Japan about agriculture, particularly those that seem to reflect non-economic considerations that are not easily explained by standard political economy approaches. The chapter concludes by arguing that a greater awareness of certain basic assumptions is necessary for a fuller explanation of how Japan's agricultural trade policy can be considered rational for voters.

3.1 Quantitative and Qualitative Rationality

The general understanding of the concept of rationality as applied in social scientific analysis suffers in part from its common usage in everyday speech. The classic essay by Regan (1978) made explicit the distinction that rationality in fact refers to two closely related concepts—qualitative rationality, and quantitative rationality. The following summarises Regan's excellent discussion of the two concepts.

Qualitative rationality is rationality in the sense of 'appropriate to the means sought.' Since this sort of rationality is defined relative to a desired outcome, it is not an end in itself and is therefore morally neutral. According to Regan, a chosen path of action can be subjectively rational (when one acts to achieve one's goal to the best of one's ability within possibly limited information), or objectively rational (in the way that is truly the best means to achieve the desired goal). Conflicts may occur, such as personal versus organisational rationality, for example in the case of a CEO who pursues a growth-maximisation strategy that benefits a company's managers over a profit-maximisation strategy that benefits shareholders. Thus, sources of conflicts of rationality arise from problems of information (as with subjective versus objective rationality), or divergence of goals (as in personal versus organisational rationality). Qualitatively irrational policy may also be pursued for emotional reasons, such as when policy reversal would cause reputational damage.

Quantitative rationality is rationality in the sense of 'what is a more as opposed to a less rational decision?', or 'what is the most rational decision in any particular case?' According to Regan, this is the form of rationality that economists typically measure. Quantitative rationality has at its fullest degree perfect rationality. In its classical definition, perfect rationality asks, (1) what is the goal?; (2) what are the alternatives?; and (3) which alternative is best? Some problems with this view include defining goals (particularly in a complex area, like policymaking), and the difficulty of making a distinction between ends and means (given that most goals are causally connected to a desire to achieve something else). Instead, an alternative approach to quantitative rationality would ask, (1) what options are available?; (2) what are the consequences of each course of action?; and (3) what is the best course of action, in light of these consequences?

Whereas qualitative rationality has not been questioned, two sorts of challenges have been made to quantitative rationality (Regan, 1978, 87). First, attempting some degree of quantitative rationality could be futile, given that it would involve a search for agreed values between policymakers and a reliance on data that is at best incomplete and at worst potentially endlessly expensive to analyse. Additionally, certain proponents of extra-rationality ('thinking outside the box') would suggest that it is sometimes necessary to go beyond traditional models of decision making in order to make policy innovations.

3.2 Rationality in Economics and Political Science

Rationality in economics

As Regan observed, economists seek to measure quantitative rationality, in the sense of measuring 'what is a more as opposed to a less rational decision?' The same holds for political economists and political scientists who employ related methodologies. In economics in particular, rational public policy is considered to be that which maximises public welfare given finite resources. For example, if two education policy options, A and B, would respectively fund 1000 or 1100 elementary school places for the same amount of expenditure, *ceteris paribus*, then policy B would clearly be more rational. But if the two policy options were C and D, which would respectively fund either 200 extra high school places or 20 extra university places, the choice is more complex. Here, questions of values immediately arise: is it better to provide wider access to intermediate education to more children, or would society benefit more from the addition of a small number of more highly educated individuals?

Such a calculation requires a metric to enable cross-case comparison. In economics, the chosen metric is *welfare*. While welfare can also include such considerations as consumption goods, leisure time, and a clean living environment—'goods' between which individuals must make trade-offs—in practice, the reference metric is always given in monetary terms, since any other measure would be too unwieldy to use. Thus, *within economics, policies are evaluated in terms of expected welfare benefits, as measured in monetary terms*. If policy option C above would raise the total lifetime earnings of the 200 secondary school pupils by, for example, $50,000 each (for a total of $10 million), and policy option D would raise total lifetime earnings of the 20 university students by $550,000 each (for a total of $11 million), the economically rational policy choice would be policy option D, since this results in higher aggregate welfare.

Admittedly, the two policy choice scenarios are simplifications that depend on certain unstated assumptions, such as the inherent comparability of different policy choices and the achievability of each policy proposal as posited. However, making these simplifying assumptions allows for a clear policy choice to be made: one can now choose between apples and oranges.

This capacity to make categorically distinct policy options readily comparable is one of the reasons that economics approaches are so analytically powerful. Transposed to the national level, the economists' view of a rational policy programme is typically one which maximises national economic welfare, as measured by Gross Domestic Product.

Rationality in political science

For scholars of the political economy of Japan who apply rational choice-based theories (e.g. Ramseyer and Rosenbluth, 1993, 1995), the economic approach described above largely holds. Rational choice theory employs rationality in the quantitative sense, and was developed out of the economic model of politics articulated by Anthony Downs in *An Economic Theory of Democracy* (1957). Downs offered two main hypotheses. First, politicians are assumed to be motivated by the aim of maximising votes, since political power can only be achieved by winning elections. Second, voters are assumed to act rationally. In this market-based model, political leaders design policy packages that maximise their chances of gaining or staying in power. Individuals and groups who would expect to gain from a certain policy will lobby for it until the expected net benefits of further expenditure is zero, while those expecting to lose from a policy will lobby against it until the expected marginal net return is zero (Anderson, 1986, 3).

Central to the Downsian model is the concept of *ideology*, which is defined as "a verbal image of the good society and the chief means of constructing such a society" (Downs, 1957, 96). If a graph of voters' ideology has a single-peaked curve (representing a clustering of voter opinion around a centrist position), a stable government could be formed in a representative two-party democratic system by parties designing policies to appeal to the median voter, and hence capturing a majority of votes. If the ideology graph curve is double-peaked (indicating that voters are split between liberal and conservative ideologies), achieving a stable majority becomes more difficult, as gaining consensus with voters on the left peak alienates voters on the right peak, and vice versa.

Although derived from economic theory, the Downsian approach complicates the idea of quantitative rationality as discussed above. Politicians and parties are no longer considered to be designing policies rationally in the economic sense of aiming to maximise national *welfare*. Rather, policy programmes here are rational if they are constructed on the basis of maximising *votes* by appealing to the median voter, who in turn is influenced by an *ideological* view of the good society, and the means to achieve this.

Other scholars of the political economy of Japan eschew theory-based approaches in favour of more traditional political science explanations. Some focus on aspects of the role of interest groups and collective action problems (following Olson, 1965), others on the role of institutions such as bureaucracies, or other factors. For example, in contrasting her approach to rational choice scholars, Aurelia George Mulgan articulates an approach in which:

> societal groupings (defined in terms of their membership of particular political, institutional, social or economic organisations or categories) are broadly conceived as pursuing their interests in politics; and the extent to which the interests of any particular societal grouping are realised will depend on the relative power of these group. This approach encapsulates a traditional, political science perspective that defines the focus of analysis in terms of interests and power which are assumed to be multifaceted and multidimensional" (Mulgan, 2000, 37).

Irrespective of the explanatory framework employed by a scholar, one point is clear: once the subject of analysis has shifted from the maximisation of the public interest (as considered in purely economic terms, such as national economic welfare) to the maximisation of *specified private interests* (such as maximising votes received by a party of the benefits to a given interest group or institution), the application of the idea of quantitative rationality to public policy analysis must be reconsidered. Quantitative rationality is premised on analysing the most rational way to achieve a goal, but in shifting from economics to political economy and political science, the goal—or, in economic terms, the *maximand*—has changed.

Where does this leave the analysis of rational public policy? It seems that any analysis of rational policy cannot escape the value dimension. As such, prior to answering the question 'what is a more as opposed to a less rational decision?' (which is the domain of economics), one must always answer the question: *what is the maximand?* And defining this inescapably involves values. In philosophical terms, this requires a shift from a purely positive question to a normative one.

The following section makes the argument that normative assumptions are deeply and silently embedded in contemporary mainstream economics. The aim is not to criticise the economics approach so much as to contextualise it. By excavating these assumptions, one can situate them in a broader framework of enquiry, and in so doing shed new light on the political economy of agriculture in Japan.

3.3 Uncovering Embedded Analytical Assumptions

As a rule of thumb, the philosophical framework within which most mainstream neoclassical economists work is rarely outlined. The unstated assumption is that economics as commonly practiced is *positive economics*, dealing with the impartial analysis of matters of fact. However, since the standard metric of comparison in economics is welfare, this already implies that economic welfare is being ideologically privileged over alternative possible metrics or goals, such as the effect that any given policy would have on political rights, social equality, or health outcomes. Viewed this way, welfare-based analyses can and perhaps must also be considered in terms of their *normative* content—that is, with regard to the values that shape the basic assumptions that frame economic analyses and the policy proposals for which such analyses form the basis.

Hausman and McPherson (2006) given a useful explication of this, outlining a seven-part "Moral Framework of Normative Economics" that analyses the underlying assumptions of welfare economics (distinguished from positive economics). According to the authors, economists typically assume *explanatory individualism*, meaning that "fundamental explanatory principles or laws (apart from the laws of the natural sciences) should concern the preferences, beliefs and choices of individual human beings" (2006, 234). Economists also assume that human beings are *rational* (in the sense of their preferences are complete and transitive),[36] and that they are *materially self-interested*, in that they prefer more commodities to fewer and more wealth to less (2006, 234-6). Normative economics is also committed to *ethical individualism*, a moral view which prioritises the wellbeing of individuals rather than that of social groupings, and holds that social entities have no intrinsic moral importance but only have instrumental moral importance, in cases when they serve the interests of individuals (2006, 237).

These assumptions produce a view that holds that *only individual welfare is important*. Rather than equating it to sensations of pleasure (as Jeremy Bentham took it to mean) or happiness (as J.S. Mill understood it), normative economists take *welfare* to mean the *satisfaction of preferences* (Hausman and McPherson, 2006, 238). Welfare is thus subjectively defined by the individual themselves, such that an individual who desires to smoke

TABLE 3-1: THE MORAL FRAMEWORK OF NORMATIVE ECONOMICS

1. What should economists appraise?
   a. *Outcomes
   b. Processes

2. What method(s) should economists use?
   a. *Single method of appraisal
   b. Multiple ethical perspectives, depending on problem

3. What matters about outcomes?
   a. *Consequences for individuals
   b. Consequences for groups or the environment

4. Which features of outcomes for individuals matter?
   a. *Welfare
   b. Freedom
   c. Rights
   d. Justice

5. What is welfare?
   a. *The satisfaction of preferences
   b. Some mental state, such as happiness
   c. "Objective" goods; e.g. achievements, personal relations, health, etc

6. How does welfare (as preference satisfaction) bear on the evaluation of outcomes?
   a. *Market evaluation and Pareto concepts
   b. Add up preference satisfaction

7. What role do other ethical notions play?
   a. *Independent: important, but not a concern of economics
   b. Their importance is derivable from their consequences for welfare
   c. Must be integrated into the economic appraisal
   d. Of no importance

Source: Hausman and McPherson (2006, 230).
Note: the assumptions of welfare/normative economics are highlighted with an asterisk.

cigarettes is thus satisfying her preferences—and maximising her welfare—by smoking, regardless of the effects on her health.

Hausman and McPherson argue that this identification of welfare with preference satisfaction makes meaningful interpersonal comparisons of welfare effectively impossible. An individual's utility function is constructed by ranking their preferences—an *ordinal ranking* (as in, a simple ranked list), which is entirely arbitrary, and does not represent the relative strength of preference for different items on that list. An ordinal utility function means that "utility differences could not be compared even for a single individual, and utilities could never be added or subtracted or compared across individuals" (2006, 239). As such, by focusing solely on this one consideration—welfare, understood as the satisfaction of preferences, as ranked in ordinal terms—economists forgo other moral considerations that an individual might have, such as conceptions of freedom, political rights, or justice.

In short, as summarised in Table 3-1, this moral framework of normative economics thus holds that (1) economists appraise outcomes, not processes; (2) only a single method of appraisal is to be used; (3) what is of primary importance is the consequences for individuals, rather than consequences for social groups or the environment; (4) the primarily important outcome is welfare, rather than other considerations (like freedom, rights, or justice); (5) welfare is the satisfaction of preferences; (6) welfare is evaluated by market evaluation and Pareto concepts of preference optimality; and (7) other ethical notions are independent and not a concern of economists.

This account of the underlying moral framework of normative economics has at least two important implications for policy studies. The first is that normative economics is an approach focused on individual welfare satisfaction, where this welfare is defined as the satisfaction of subjectively-defined and ordinally ranked preferences. The second is that normative economics does not engage with outcomes for groups or outcomes for individuals other than welfare, such as concerns for ethical considerations like freedom, rights, and justice. If such concerns are articulated by an individual, they are then by definition *non-economic* in nature, and cannot be incorporated into an economic calculation that deals only with welfare. Thus, any policy proposals denominated in terms of economic welfare must be evaluated in terms of these assumptions and the limitations they imply, particularly when broader conceptions of individual, societal, national, or international welfare are also being considered.

An important qualification to this must be added, concerning the increasing heterodoxy of economic analysis. Whilst economic welfare in monetary terms is certainly the globally predominant denominator in economics, other approaches have been developed. One is the Human Development Index developed by Mahbub ul Haq, Amartya Sen, and others, and now calculated annually by the United Nations Development Programme. This index considers life expectancy, years of schooling, and per capita Gross National Income at purchasing power parity. A second is the Gross National Happiness concept originated by the government of Bhutan, which attempts to estimate aspects of sustainable development, cultural values, environmental conservation, and good governance. Third, behavioural economists including Daniel Kahneman have suggested advanced methodologies for measuring happiness, while other quantitative methods for measuring a concept like Gross National Happiness are also possible. None of these denominators are without their problems, and any measure that is based on ordinal ranking is subject to the same limitations discussed above. However, the existence of such alternatives does demonstrate the possibility of economics-based analyses that go beyond the limitations of the welfare economics approach.

The utilization of economic welfare in analysis does not require that all economists who use it subscribe to the moral position outlined above. Non-economic factors do of course matter even to economists, but the difficulties of quantifying such factors in an objective fashion mean that they are generally not employed in such fields as trade economics or agricultural economics. Thus, welfare remains the standard unit of account in economic analyses, including for analyses related to agricultural and trade policies, and non-economic considerations are not incorporated into analyses in such research fields.

3.4 Non-economic Ideas about Agriculture: Preliminary Evidence

There is substantial preliminary evidence to suggest that non-economic considerations may be central to the way that many Japanese people think about agriculture in general, and most especially about rice agriculture. If true, such non-economic factors could be shaping the policy preferences of voters and consumers with regard to agricultural policy, but would not be included in—or even analysable by—the typical methods of analysis usually applied in the study of the political economy of Japan. Such non-economic considerations are evidenced in texts and images found in a range of sources, including academia, political communications, and the media.

Scholars of Japan in other fields have long argued for the importance of non-economic factors. Writing about general economic attitudes in the 1980s, when a revisionist view of Japan as an interventionist, protectionist, and mercantilist state was common, the sociologist Ronald Dore contended that Japanese people rejected free market principles, and that they did so for both moral and practical reasons. According to Dore (1986, 1), the Japanese "don't believe in the invisible hand. They believe... that you cannot get a decent moral society, not even an efficient society, simply out of the mechanisms of the market powered by the motivational fuel of self-interest, however clever, or even divinely inspired, those mechanisms may be. The morality has got to come from the hearts, the wills and motives, of the individuals in it."

In contrast to Adam Smith's dictum that we expect our dinner from the self-interest rather than the benevolence of the butcher and the baker, Dore argued that Japanese people think that "[t]he butcher and the baker have *got* to be benevolent. They need to have a conscience about the quality of the meat and the bread they sell. They need to care" (1986, 1; emphasis in original). Caring was both a duty and also the best policy in the long run. For example, a business who stuck with a supplier in difficulty even when lower-priced competitors were available created a moral obligation that would be repaid if they themselves ever experienced trouble. This also created a particular approach to economic policy, namely a belief that sometimes oligopoly should be adopted for technical-efficient reasons, that stable employment practices create better-quality human relations, and that the realities of international competition require state intervention (1986, 6).

A notable political statement of this kind of moral economic view came in a 2009 essay "A New Path for Japan" by Hatoyama Yukio of the Democratic Party of Japan (DPJ), one month before he became prime minister, which articulated a harsh critique of the "U.S.-led movement... usually called globalization."[37] According to Hatoyama, the "winds of market fundamentalism" had "buffeted" post-Cold War Japan; this form of capitalism treated people "not as an end but as a means" leading to a loss of "human dignity"; and "unrestrained market fundamentalism" was "void of morals or moderation."[38] Referencing the French Revolution, Hatoyama advocated the concept of *yūai*, which he translated as 'fraternity' and defined as "a principle that aims to adjust to the excesses of the current globalized brand of capitalism and accommodate the local economic practices that have been fostered through our traditions". The essay continued:

> The economic order in any country is built up over long years and reflects the influence of traditions, habits and national lifestyles. But globalism has progressed without any regard for non-economic values, or for environmental issues or problems of resource restriction... If we look back on the changes in Japanese society since the end of the Cold War, I believe it is no exaggeration to say that the global economy has damaged traditional economic activities and destroyed local communities... In terms of market theory, people are simply personnel expenses. But in the real world people support the fabric of the local community and are the physical embodiment of its lifestyle, traditions and culture. An individual gains respect as a person by acquiring a job and a role within the local community and being able to maintain his family's livelihood... Under the principle of fraternity, we would not implement policies that leave areas relating to human lives and safety—such as agriculture, the environment and medicine—to the mercy of globalism... Our responsibility as politicians is to refocus our attention on those non-economic values that have been thrown aside by the march of globalism. We must work on policies that regenerate the ties that bring people together, that take greater account of nature and the environment, that rebuild welfare and medical systems, that provide better education and child-rearing support, and that address wealth disparities.[39]

Throughout the New Path essay, Hatoyama articulates a vision of the domestic economy and society that emphasises (1) non-economic values such as traditions, habits, and lifestyles; (2) the dangers of unregulated markets; (3) the negative social impact of external forces like globalisation; and (4) the need for government intervention to protect the livelihoods and address income inequality. Given its place in modern Japan's political economy, it is also entirely consistent that Hatoyama should include agriculture as one of three areas that should not be left to the "mercy of globalization."

Other prime ministers have also stressed the importance of agricultural and rural communities more directly. One example is Tanaka Kakuei, often seen as the father of the vast public works projects that transformed the nation's infrastructure and countryside, for better or worse. Shortly before becoming prime minister in summer 1972, he published *Nippon Rettō Kaizō-ron* (republished in English as *Building a New Japan: A Plan for Remodelling the Japanese Archipelago*). In this book, Tanaka described rural Japan as the wellspring of the modern nation and a source of pride that he sought to restore economically:

> Those born in the [Meiji and Taishō] eras[40] have a deep sense of love and pride in their native locales. While life in these rural villages may not have

> been rich, it was home. Home was the place where your stern father and gentle mother lived, where you could always find your childhood friends, and whose green fields, rolling hills, and fresh streams remained with you forever. Seeking their fortunes, village youths left their ancestral homes for faraway cities… Whatever their fate, whether in success or failure, they always remembered the people and scenes of their unchanging homeplace… I believe that the endless fountain of energy which has built today's Japan derives from the cherished and respected rural homes from which all of us have originally come.[41]

The significance of agriculture has often been noted in academic studies. The political scientist Adam Sheingate argued that "the cultural resonance of agriculture is very strong in Japan… For many Japanese, urban and rural alike, the ceremonies and traditions surrounding rice cultivation hark back to a simpler, pre-industrial time when individuals were closely tied to their communities through reciprocity and mutual dependence. Farmers embody these values. As in France, agricultural policy is viewed as a public good that serves the entire political community rather than the particular interests of a small group of producers" (Sheingate, 2000, 187).

One visual representation that evidences the cultural resonance of agriculture is shown in Figure 3-1, the cover-image from Abe Shinzō's personal Facebook social network page, as it appeared from around 2014 until 2020. The photograph depicts the prime minister bowing deeply to an elderly rice farmer. It is reasonable to assume that, of all the images that Abe or his staff could have selected, this image showing reverence to a farmer was chosen strategically for its resonance with voters. The fact that the image remained in use throughout Abe's premiership also speaks to the enduring importance of what is being portrayed.

FIG. 3-1: COVER IMAGE FROM ABE SHINZŌ'S FACEBOOK PAGE

Within agriculture in Japan, the most totemic product is rice. The sacred connotation of the term *sei'iki* is stronger for rice than for any of the other items it refers to. The economic historian Penelope Francks (2007) noted rice's religious, historical, and symbolic significance, and argued that it became associated with status and sophistication in the Tokugawa period before spreading as a mass-consumed food in the nineteenth-century, and that it took on new meaning in relation to national identity in the turbulent 1920s and 1930s. The cultural anthropologist Katarzyna Cwiertka has described the role of the army in spreading the consumption of rice as a daily staple in the Meiji era by supplying it to peasant soldiers who would continue to demand it after returning to their homes. The 1942 Food Control Act was also significant since it "granted all Japanese the right, even if only in theory, to a rice-centred diet" (Cwiertka, 2007, 131).

In a richly detailed work entitled *Rice As Self* (1993), the cultural anthropologist Emiko Ohnuki-Tierney explicitly argues that attitudes to rice in Japan cannot be understood solely in economic terms. Ohnuki-Tierney contends that, "from a cultural perspective the argument about rice in contemporary Japan demonstrates beyond doubt that, for the Japanese, rice is not simply a good to fill the stomach. Japanese attitudes and behaviours towards rice are not governed by economic rationale. The rice importation issue, which has a political dimension, is based on broader cultural issues involving the meaning of rice. An understanding of rice in Japan requires an understanding of the broader cultural and historical landscape in which the meanings of rice and rice agriculture are embedded" (Ohnuki-Tierney, 1993, 29).

Ohnuki-Tierney argues that rice is a "dominant symbol" that occurs frequently or conspicuously and serves as a window to reveal something about culture (1993, 5), and that rice and rice paddies are metaphors that Japanese people use in defining their identity in relation to others (1993, 4). Her study also examines the role of rice in a Japanese creation myth, and explores the fact that rice was understood to have a soul in Japan's traditional, animistic religion Shintō (1993, 45ff). This soul of the rice grain was called *ina dama* or *inadamashii* and identified as a deity (*kami*), with the name *Uka-no-Kami*. For Ohnuki-Tierney, throughout Japanese history, rice represented power, beauty, the good life, and was a sacred gift. Rice paddies represented "our land" (1993, 81), and ultimately "rice paddies also stand for the Japanese nation itself" (1993, 98).

In politics, ideas about the non-economic importance of agriculture were frequently articulated in policy debates after Japan entered into negotiations for the Trans Pacific Partnership, which opponents feared would result in a high degree of agricultural liberalisation. One example was an opinion piece that appeared on the front page of the Asahi Shimbun newspaper on October 30, 2013 under the title *Mizuho no Kuni no Shimpai Goto* ('Concern in the country of rice plants').[42] It begins:

> In Japan, the expression "eating rice from the same pot" means camaraderie. I have never heard anyone say "eating pasta from the same pot." In Japan, which is also called "Mizuho no Kuni" (country of vigorous rice plants), every single grain of rice has been part of people's daily life and culture for thousands of years… Rice seedlings are planted in the spring, absorb abundant water during the rainy season and make paddies lush with green in the summer. In the autumn, golden ears of rice plants ripple in the wind. Many people feel spiritual attachment to the beautiful landscape of rice paddies spreading across the rich Japanese land. Prime Minister Shinzo Abe described the sight of terraced rice paddies as "breathtakingly beautiful." Many people must feel the same way.[43]

Regarding the TPP negotiations, the author suggests (in language reminiscent of Hatoyama) that they mean that rice farmers "will be thrown into the boundless ocean of competition based on the free market mechanism." The article continues, "Many people say it cannot be helped, but I find it questionable. Since the numbers tell all in the economy, the intangible contributions of rice agriculture to such factors as history, culture, landscape and the ecosystem are not considered as exchangeable values. I am worried that Japan may lose an important asset in order to compete with foreign-grown rice."

The article also quotes the words of Hisashi Inoue, a popular Japanese writer and the author of *Kome no Hanashi* ('Rice Tales'), who wrote that," rice paddies are excellent public assets, and rice is an important product that plays a key role in Japan's safety and security." Giving a sense of the wider meaning attached to agriculture, the final paragraph discusses the kanji used for writing 'rice,' which can be broken down into the characters for the number '88,' symbolising the many steps of hard work required to grow rice. The piece concludes that "[r]ice symbolizes subtle Japanese tradition and culture. But in this age of globalization, agriculture needs to be efficient. Would it be too much to ask for the latter without losing the former?"[44]

Taken together, this diverse sample of political, historical, anthropological and media sources provide sufficient basis to suggest that it *might* be the case that the popular view of agriculture in Japan is that it is something special and unique, and that its value lies primarily in non-economic aspects. It is not necessary for political economists to accept in full the arguments of sociologists, cultural anthropologists, politicians or media writers to see that *ideas* about agriculture may carry a strong cultural resonance for Japanese people, and that in turn, these ideas may be important factors that influence the policy preferences of voters. This possibility offers a solid reason to undertake a more detailed study of ideas in the political economy of Japanese agriculture.

******

This chapter has explored issues relating to rationality and its application in the fields of public policy, economics, and political science. It has also examined the philosophical assumptions of the standard welfare economics approach to policy studies, shown how non-economic values are not analysable within this framework, and offered preliminary evidence for the significance of non-economic ideas in relation to agriculture and agricultural trade liberalisation in Japan.

In the discussion of rationality, it was seen that qualitative rationality is not challenged conceptually, though it may be difficult to choose rational actions due to issues of imperfect information and the divergence of goals. Quantitative rationality aims ultimately at perfect rationality, but is open to critiques such as the implicit prior need to decide on an agreed goal. Economists and rational choice-based political scientists, among others, aim at quantitative rationality. In simple terms, economically rational policy is that which maximises welfare, denominated in monetary terms.

Within the economics approach, certain clearly rational choices can be identified, provided that simplifying assumptions are made. However, once these assumptions are relaxed, questions of values soon enter the analysis. Political economists and political scientists would consider a rational policy platform as one that allows a politician or party to get elected. However, the goal at which such policies are now aiming has already shifted, meaning that the standard concept of rationality can no longer be applied in policy analysis.

Welfare-focused economists, while aiming at positive, fact-oriented methods of enquiry implicitly make certain philosophical assumptions, including explanatory individualism, individual rationality, material self-interest, and ethical individualism. Welfare is taken to mean the satisfaction of preferences, which are understood as subjectively decided and ordinally ranked. This allows for cross-case comparison within the assumed welfare framework but effectively precludes true inter-personal—or even *intra*-personal—comparison due to the impossibility of comparing ordinal utility preferences. Likewise, this approach prevents a comparison of other outcome considerations, such as freedom, rights, or justice. Heterodox approaches to economics also exist, which aim to capture broader measures like human development and happiness, though these approaches too may have methodological issues.

With respect to Japanese agriculture, there is evidence from a variety of sources to indicate the possibility that ideas held about agriculture reflect non-economic values. Examples from academia, political texts, and the media together suggest that agriculture in general and rice agriculture in particular are perceived as having inherent value that go beyond their role in the economy. This possibility has been articulated in a number of ways, with reference to culture, identity, societal values, aesthetics, and history, among others. Specific ideas cited about the importance of agriculture relate to its cultural and religious significance, the perceived historical role of agriculture as the source of the nation and national vigour, the wellbeing and livelihoods of farmers as an important section of society, the limitations of markets and the need for government intervention, the protection of the environment, the role of rice in creating beautiful landscapes, and the contribution of agriculture to the safety and security of Japan.

Just as with the term *sei'iki*, political speech in praise of agriculture may be no more than a strategic linguistic manoeuvre by political actors with vested interests. However, if such speech resonates with the views and values held by voters generally, this would offer further confirmation of agriculture's special status and of the role of these ideas in shaping agricultural policy preferences.

The preliminary evidence presented in this chapter indicates that this may indeed be the case. If this is so, how might that effect be meaningfully theorised and analysed in social scientific terms? The next chapter outlines ways in which the roles of ideas have been incorporated into other strands of economics, political science, and political economy literature, including with regard to agriculture. It then presents a conceptual framework for analysing the role of ideas in policy preference formation in the political economy of agriculture in Japan.

CHAPTER 4

HOW IDEAS SHAPE POLICY PREFERENCES

The premise of this study is that ideas are among the significant variables that explain the persistence of agricultural support and protection in Japan, and that ideational factors have not been sufficiently incorporated into the dominant, interest-based accounts of Japan's agricultural policy regime. The preliminary evidence presented in Chapter 3 suggests that agriculture may be considered as somehow different and special, and that the views of both policymakers and the public may be influenced by non-economic ideas. That chapter also showed how political economy approaches based on calculations of economic welfare struggle to account for non-economic maximands, due to embedded assumptions.

This chapter considers how ideas have been incorporated into four existing strands of literature—rational choice theory, historical institutionalism, constructivism, and new political economy—and posits how each of those approaches would theorise the case of Japanese agricultural policy. It then develops an original conceptual framework for incorporating ideas as an explanatory variable for policy preferences in the political economy of agriculture in Japan.

4.1 Defining and Using the Concept of Ideas

What is an idea, how is it studied in social science, and what ontological and epistemological implications are involved in its utilisation as an explanatory variable? As with the concept of rationality, attempts to define an idea can suffer from the word's broad vernacular usage, and the resulting lack of clarity or consensus can have consequences when ideas are used analytically. For example, some scholars take ideas as one subset of ideational factors, a category which could also include identities, norms, aspirations and ideologies (Ruggie, 1998, 855). Others see worldviews, norms, identities, values, intellectual beliefs, and culture as examples of ideas (Campbell, 2004, 90).

The definition of idea itself tends to vary with the theoretical approach of the scholar. Broadly speaking, for rational choice theorists, ideas are considered *beliefs held by individuals*. Goldstein and Keohane (1993) classified three types of ideational beliefs: *world views* that are embedded in the symbolism of a culture and deeply affect modes of thought and discourse; *principled beliefs* that are normative ideas specifying criteria for distinguishing right and wrong; and *causal beliefs* about cause and effect that gain authority from a shared consensus among recognised elites.

Ideas are also considered as *world views* by historical institutionalists. Hall (1993, 279) defined ideas in terms of the interpretive framework that specifies policy goals, the instruments used to attain them, and even the nature of the problems to be addressed. For Skogstad (1998), ideas were "mental constructions that encapsulate common beliefs and valued norms, for example about the economy and polity and the role of the individual within them [that] underpin all policies."

For organisational institutionalists and constructivists, ideas are commonly considered as *cultural norms*, that is, socially constituted webs of connected ideas. Peter Katzenstein (1996, ix) defined norms as "social facts" that "typically inform how political actors define what they want to accomplish." They include *regulative norms* that "help coordinate political conflicts" and *constitutive norms* that "shape political conflicts over identity". Other constructivists, such as Daniel Béland and Robert Henry Cox (2011, 3) define ideas as *causal beliefs* produced in the mind, which posit connections between things and between people in the world in formal or informal ways, and which also provide guides for action.

In social science analysis, ideas can be utilised in two ways, either as a *dependent variable* endogenous to the model, or an *independent variable* that is exogenous. As a dependent variable, ideas are strategies used by political actors to help achieve their goals. An example of this would be the ideology of Marxism-Leninism used by Soviet elites to gain and maintain political power, or the idea of free trade and liberalisation when used by certain elites in liberal democracies to advance their own interests. Considered as a dependent variable, ideas are used instrumentally and cynically and have no inherent meaning.

Taken as an independent variable, ideas can shape or determine the preferences of political actors. In this understanding, ideas have inherent meaning for actors, who genuinely believe in them and whose preferences or actions are to some extent influenced by them. The necessity to distinguish between instrumental behaviour and sincere belief makes the study of ideas as an independent variable methodologically a more challenging—and less common—undertaking.

For this reason, examining ideas as a fully independent variable is not a straightforward task.[45] Often, ideas are studied in terms of how they interact with interests and institutions (Skogstad, 1998, 464). How ideas are operationalised in practice in social science also depends upon the ontological and methodological positions adopted by the scholar. As Gofas and Hay (2010, 15-16) discuss, there are important ontological and epistemological debates around the use of ideas.

In ontological terms, the main question concerns the relationship between material and ideational factors. Rational choice theorists adopt a simple *ontological dualism* that draws a clear, Cartesian distinction between the two. Constructivists and others adopt a more complex *ontological duality* that stresses that the two concepts are not ontologically distinct. Within this position, some stress *ontic duality,* namely that both material factors and ideas have real existence, while others stress *analytical duality*, the view that the distinction is a mental construction rather than reflecting social reality.

In epistemological terms, the main debate relates to the difference between causal logics (meaning mechanistic causality) versus constituent logics (meaning logical or conceptual enablement). In short, those adopting causal logics see ideas as an independent variable whose effects are mechanistic and autonomous. Those adopting constituent logics see ideas as providing the conditions that make possible a "social or political event, behaviour or effect" (Gofas and Hay, 2010, 16).

4.2 Applying Four Ideational Approaches to the Case of Japan

The following examines how ideas have been applied as variables in policy studies in four relevant strands of literature: rational choice theory, historical institutionalism, organisational institutionalism or constructivism, and new political economy. After outlining each approach, we posit how that approach would seek to explain the case of agriculture in the political economy of Japan.

Ideas in rational choice theory: from ideology to auxiliary variable

Despite rational choice theory's central focus on how material interests determine behaviour, ideas have been incorporated into rational choice policy studies implicitly or explicitly in a number of ways. Indeed, Gofas and Hay (2010, 18) observe that "by far the most influential attempt to 'take ideas seriously' has come from within" rational choice theory. An ideational element was present in the original Downsian economic model of the political marketplace, and more recently has been at the centre of other choice-theoretic accounts of politics.

Ideology was defined briefly by Downs (1957) as "a verbal image of the good society and the chief means of constructing such a society." The concept was used sceptically. Ideologies were nearly always viewed in contemporary political science as "a means to political power employed by social classes or other groups, rather than as mere representations of actual goals"; they were not accepted at face-value because they were "tainted with their espousers' desire to gain power" (Downs, 1957, 96). Downs constructed an intentionally "oversimplified" spatial model of a left-right ideological spectrum based on preferred levels of government intervention in the economy (1957, 139). Ideologies were useful to rational voters as time-saving devices who used them as a proxy for examining a political party's position on a multitude of issues. For voters who were ideologically driven, ideologies were the main consideration in voting. For parties, ideologies offered a way to appeal to a broad selection of voters, and had the benefit of being vague and variable. Parties competed with each other to maximise vote share by differentiating themselves in terms of ideologies.

Clearly, this is a very thin view of the role of ideas in politics. It treats ideologies as purely instrumental for parties and most voters (albeit with apparent inherent value for ideological voters), and offers no explanation of the origins of ideologies or the ideas that presumably constitute them, nor does it model *how* ideologies might influence either voters or politicians who seek and exercise power. Ideational differences are outside the model: ideas are simply assumed, and not demonstrated in any way. In the words of Shepsle (1985, 233), ideas were no more than "hooks on which politicians hang their objectives and by which they further their interests."

Yet what is noteworthy is not that ideas were not dealt with *well* by Downs, but that even this most simplified economic model of politics included a significant ideational element. This seems to be at least an implicit admission that ideas *do* matter, distinct from material interests, in some analytically important way. The inclusion of a specific category of ideological voters further implies that there are some individuals for whom ideational factors trump material interests.

In the decades after Downs, ideas became marginal in social scientific enquiry. Béland and Cox (2011, 6) argue that ideas developed a "beleaguered status, often derided as imprecise or placed lower in status than material interests as motives for political and social action." Instead, the preferred subjects for social scientific analysis were material interests and institutions (rules, conventions, and practices). This was in part due to the rise of behaviourism, which eschewed interpretive methods of enquiry on methodological grounds, and the rise of neo-Marxism, which dismissed non-materialist explanations of human behaviour.

However, towards the end of the twentieth century, rational institutionalist theorists began to utilise ideas once again as a variable to explain cases in which materialist explanations failed to predict observed outcomes. Arising from the work of Douglass North and Oliver Williamson, rational institutionalism argues that institutions were built to advance the self-interest of actors. It continues to embrace methodological individualism (with individual actions giving rise to institutions) and the assumption that individual self-interest motivates actors, subject to the availability of relevant information and actors' cognitive abilities (Campbell, 2004, 14).

The most influential statement of ideas in rational institutionalism is Judith Goldstein and Robert Keohane's work, *Ideas in Foreign Policy.* As noted above, this approach considered ideas in terms of world views, principled beliefs, and causal beliefs. Ideas were important because they "help to clarify the principles and connections of causal relationships and to coordinate individual behaviour" (Goldstein and Keohane, 1993, 5). Ideas could be influential by providing road maps for actors to realise their interests, as focal points for helping choose between multiple Pareto-optimal equilibria outcomes, or by becoming embedded in institutions and shaping policy outcomes in the absence of innovation.

One criticism of this approach is that Goldstein and Keohane essentially privilege material factors and resort to ideas as an auxiliary variable only when material explanations fail (Gofas and Hay, 2010). Evidence of this includes Goldstein and Keohane's null hypothesis, that "variation in policy across countries, or over time, is entirely accounted for by changes in factors *other than* ideas" (Goldstein and Keohane, 1993, 6). Similarly, in a study of U.S. trade policy, Goldstein (1989) calculates the outcomes actors' interests would have implied, compares that to the actual outcomes, and attributes the residual to the influence of ideas. A more general criticism is that rational choice theory is articulated as a positivist approach, but if ideas are necessary for individuals to conceive of their interests, as Goldstein and Keohane hold, and if ideas can vary between societies (as they surely do), then it follows that material interests can no longer be a reliable basis for predictive theory.

Applied to the case of agricultural policy in Japan, an ideational rational institutionalist approach after Goldstein and Keohane[46] might argue that (1) the idea of agricultural support and protection was adopted by postwar politicians because it helped achieve electoral goals; (2) among a number of Pareto-optimum policy outcomes, the idea of agricultural protection offered one option, and was employed as a way to decide policy; and (3) the idea of agricultural protection became deeply embedded in institutions like the agricultural ministry and the hegemonic LDP government, and continued to shape policy in the absence of policy innovation, at least until the 2000s when Japan started pursuing an FTA strategy.

Ideas in historical institutionalism: policy paradigms

Historical institutionalism has roots in the work of Karl Marx and Max Weber, and was developed by political scientists focusing on how decision-making is affected by the arrangement of institutions of the state (government agencies, parliament etc), the institutional arrangement of economies (such as labour unions and business associations), and the institutional connections between states and economies (including economic policies, regulation of business, and property rights) (Campbell, 2004, 23). Whereas behaviouralism in the 1950s and 1960s explained political outcomes through reference to the behaviours and actions of leading individuals, historical institutionalists focused on the origins, impacts, and changes of institutions. In the 1990s, several scholars in this tradition began exploring the role of ideas in institutions.

Notably, Peter Hall (1993) developed a model of policymaking taking place within an ideational *paradigm* characterised by social learning. Adapting Thomas Kuhn's theory of scientific paradigms, Hall argued that three orders of change exist in policymaking. First-order changes are day-to-day adjustments in policies such as varying interest rates, while second-order changes are changes in the instruments used to implement policy. Third-order changes are changes in the overall policy framework or ideology within which policymaking takes place, such as the shift from a Keynesian to a monetarist approach to macroeconomic policy. Third-order changes equate to Kuhnian paradigm shifts. Since paradigms are never fully commensurable in scientific or technical terms, the process of paradigm shifts was likely to come from sociological rather than scientific grounds. Hall argued that a policy paradigm generates "long periods of continuity punctuated occasionally by the disjunctive experience of paradigm shift" (1993, 291).

In this view, paradigms have the greatest impact in institutional settings, where policymaking is done by experts or long-tenured administrators, so that the paradigms are "likely to become intertwined with firmly established operating procedures and departmental routines" (Hall, 1993, 291). In some cases, these will amount to "fully elaborated paradigms", whereas in others they will be more like a loose "web of ideas," affecting policy but subject to frequent variations. Even in the latter case, an "overarching set of ideas" may have a role, since even cynical, self-interested bureaucrats and politicians must articulate their actions in terms that will receive popular support, seem consistent, and motivate those who will implement the policies. In addition, actions invariably reflect a particular understanding of a given policy sphere, and the "terms of discourse in which that sphere and the policies appropriate to it are discussed constrain and enable, often in highly specific ways" (Hall, 1993, 284-5). New ideas play an important role since competition takes place within both the political and bureaucratic classes in terms of finding new solutions to existing problems. Not only does the exercise of power involve social learning but so too can competition for power.

In Hall's account, policy paradigm change occurs through a process of social learning that takes place within partisan, politicised forums. Coleman et al. (1997) suggest a related trajectory for paradigm change that is extremely pertinent to the present study, being based on an analysis of agricultural policy. The authors identify an ongoing shift between two paradigms of agricultural policy, the state-assisted paradigm and the market-liberal paradigm, outlined in detail below. Coleman et al. propose that political institutions (especially policy networks) and the nature of political feedback combine to create a slower but equally decisive process of paradigm change.[47]

The state-assisted paradigm in agricultural policy has two tenets: that (1) "the agricultural sector contributes to national policy goals and therefore merits special attention", and that (2) "the price mechanism is a sub-optimal means of achieving an efficient and productive agricultural sector… [i]mperfect markets combine with unmanageable natural risks and concern for food security to give governments a large role in subsidising agricultural production" (Coleman et. al, 1997, 275). These principles gave rise to three key agricultural policy goals in OECD countries: (1) that farmers should receive sufficient farming income to ensure an adequate living standard; (2) that increased efficiency should be pursued by the adoption of new technology to allow intensive production; and (3) that marginal farmers should receive assistance to become efficient, commercially viable agricultural producers. Coleman et al. suggest that all countries had subscribed to some degree to these goals, at least in the past, and that some countries continue to organise their agricultural sectors almost entirely around them.

By the 1990s, this paradigm was in the process of giving way to an alternative, the market liberal paradigm. The market liberal paradigm focuses on market allocation and efficiency over state intervention and equity. There are four tenets of this view: (1) that agriculture should be seen as being like any other economic sector and not connected to serving other policy goals; (2) that competitive markets based only on supply and demand should determine producers' incomes; (3) that only market-competitive producers should remain active in the market; and (4) that individual producers should be responsible for insuring themselves against income loss due to natural disasters (Coleman et. al, 1997, 275-6).

After Hall and Coleman et al., an ideational historical institutionalist account of Japanese agriculture might proceed as follows.[48] A protectionist approach to agricultural policy arose in Japan in the 1930s in response to the poverty suffered by farmers in the Great Recession and because the military government came to favour rural areas for providing strong and healthy soldiers and having perceived moral superiority to cities. Through the postwar agrarian reforms and the LDP's actions to secure its rural base, a protectionist or 'state assisted' policy paradigm became embedded in successive LDP governments, the agriculture ministry, and JA. From the 1960s onwards, rice price adjustments and other supports represented first-order policy changes. The introduction of the gentan around 1970 and the partial reorientation of agricultural policy after the 1994 Uruguay Round agreement and 1999 new agricultural basic law were examples of second-order changes. Proponents of a market liberal paradigm have slowly been growing in number, particularly since the 1986 Maekawa Report and American pressure for agricultural market opening in the 1980s and 1990s. The greatest pressure for a paradigm shift has come since Japan began pursuing bilateral trade agreements in the 2000s and mega regional agreements in the 2010s. Currently, the state-assisted paradigm remains dominant but became increasingly contested during the Abe era.

Ideas in organisational institutionalism and constructivism: norms

Organisation institutionalism has roots in the work of Max Weber and Emile Durkheim. Scholars in this tradition hold that organisations do not always behave in (instrumentally) rational ways to achieve organisational goals. Instead, their behaviour may be influenced by factors in their environment. Norms and values operate as important factors shaping institutional behaviour. Thus, institutions may follow a *logic of appropriateness*, undertaking what is generally considered appropriate behaviour in their specific environment, rather than a *logic of instrumentality*, meaning adopting the most efficient means to achieve a goal. For examples, Katzenstein (1996) explains the reluctance of Japan's police and military to use physical force with reference to the norms that became embedded in these institutions after the intense political conflicts of the 1950s. More recent organisational institutionalists have stressed that actors' cognition and perceptions of appropriate behaviour can depend on such aspects as set scripts, schema, habits, and routines (see Campbell, 2004, 17-23).

Taking this out of the domestic sphere, social constructivist approaches to international relations theory hold that ideas or conceptions of interests as conceived by foreign policy actors are determined endogenously by norms, ideologies, and causal beliefs (e.g. Wendt, 1992, 1999; Ruggie, 1998). These ideational factors in turn influence state behaviour in the international sphere.

An organisational institutionalist or constructivist account of Japan's agricultural policy might proceed as follows. In the postwar era, a norm of agricultural protection and support developed. Policymakers were socialised into believing that protecting farmers was a basic duty. This duty had roots in the legal frameworks underpinning agricultural policy, such as the 1942 Food Control Act that theoretically guaranteed a rice-based diet and the 1961 Agricultural Basic Law's stipulation for reducing the rural-urban income gap. Further roots can be found in the identification of farming and rice with Japanese identity, and the identification of farming villages with traditional Japanese life. This norm of agricultural protection was so strong that agricultural protection continued despite chronic budget deficits in the sector. As many other countries have switched from protectionist to market-oriented policy regimes, Japanese politicians and bureaucrats participating in trade negotiations and in international organisations have come under the influence of peers from countries with market-oriented agricultural policies. This has contributed to a heightened awareness among policymakers of a new international norm of liberalised agricultural policies, which may be incrementally changing Japan's protectionist norm.

Ideas in the new political economy approach

Ideas as an explanatory variable have been taken seriously within new approaches in mainstream political economy in recent years (e.g. Rodrik, 2014; Mukand and Rodrik, 2018). For example, Dani Rodrik (2014, 194) argues that, "[w]hile hidden assumptions play a role in all economic models… the failure to recognise the role of ideas in shaping interests (and their pursuit) has especially serious implications in political economy." Standard rational-choice based political economy models assume that rational individuals as political agents (acting as voters, lobbies, elites, or politicians) solve well-defined optimisation problems, with at least three components: (1) an objective *preference* function, such as a consumer utility function; (2) a set of *constraints*, such as a budget constraint; and (3) a set of *choice variables*, such as the quantities of consumption to be chosen. Rodrik argues that each of these three elements implicitly assumes a set of ideas.

First, with regard to preferences, whereas microeconomic preferences relating to supply and demand can be reduced to maximising consumer surplus or producer profits in economic analyses, in the political sphere there are a variety of plausible maximands. Examples include honour, glory, reputation, respect, income, power, durability in office, and the good of the country. Rodrik posits that "[m]uch human behaviour is driven by abstract ideals, sacred values or conceptions of loyalty that cannot be reduced to economic ends" (2014, 191), adding that this viewpoint should not be controversial in an age of suicide bombings. As constructivists in political science have also noted, how individuals define themselves—in terms of social class, ethnic group, religion, nationality, profession etc—impacts crucially on how they evaluate 'self' interests and judge whether different social states advance those interests.

Second, regarding constraints, individuals' understandings of 'how the world works' are based on ideas regarding such things as the social value of home ownership. There is no guarantee that these mental models are objectively correct, as different interpretations of the 2008 global economic and financial crisis showed. Third, concerning choice variables, ideas about 'what can be done' are also important. Rather than a limited menu of policy options as traditionally described in 'overstructured' political economy models, new ideas (i.e. innovative policies) are in practice at the heart of political decision-making. Political agents "design their own strategy space" with the available policy instruments "up for grabs and limited only by their political imagination" (Rodrik, 2014, 195). New ideas can function similarly to new technology by pushing out the boundary of what is possible to produce with a given set of inputs, and can thus be characterised as a 'political transformation frontier' similar to an economic transformation constraint.

Whereas Rodrik focuses mainly on ideas as policy innovation, the concern of the present study is with the first of these aspects: the influence of ideas on preferences. Such an approach has occasionally been considered by other political economists. For example, Alesina et al (2012) considered the impact of ideas of fairness, while the influence of media on voting behaviour has also been demonstrated (DellaVigna and Kaplan, 2007). As noted in Chapter 1, Mayda and Rodrik (2005) found evidence for the impact of both economic and non-economic factors influencing trade policy preferences, while Mansfield and Mutz (2009) found evidence that out-group anxiety (isolationism and ethnocentrism) and sociotropic perceptions of trade's impact on the national economy as a whole were significant in shaping trade policy preferences in the United States.

A new political economy account of Japan's agricultural policies, after Rodrik, may contain the following elements. In the preference function of individuals with respect to agricultural policy, ideas of efficiency and cost are given a relatively low priority. Instead, ideas about issues like food safety and domestic food production are given a high priority by individuals (including voters and policymakers). Regarding constraints, the apparent success of interventionist economic policy in postwar Japan (at least until the 1990s) may have shaped mental models about 'how the world works', particularly for older individuals. Even during the subsequent years of relative economic stagnation, residual beliefs about Japan's cultural uniqueness may also have shaped individuals to think that the economic model that works in Japan is unique. Alternatively, such a view could be grounded in the country's extremely high urban population share and population density in cities, creating a view that Japan needs to balance its economy and society by supporting rural areas. Regarding choice variables, policy innovations such as linking agricultural protection and support with rural economic revitalisation or introducing the concept of multifunctionality in the 1990s may have enabled the continuation of high agricultural expenditures despite changing fiscal circumstances.

4.3 A New Framework for Ideas and Policy Preferences

This section develops a theoretical framework for incorporating ideas as an explanatory variable in the political economy of agriculture in Japan, in a manner that is communicative with previously-discussed approaches in economics, political economy, and political science. The purpose is to theorise ideas as an independent variable and policy preferences as a dependent variable. The model posits a relationship between the two with reference to the cultural and historical context of society, the values held by individuals within it, and the vectors by which each element can be transmitted.

The model takes as its unit of analysis the individual as a political agent, for three reasons. First, ideas are a social phenomenon that affect everyone in society. If ideas about the importance of agriculture in history, culture, and other areas are significant, they should be in evidence across society and not restricted to elite policy actors. Second, agricultural policy also affects every individual in a society on multiple levels: as a consumer of food, a taxpayer, and a voter, and possibly also as a farmer, a worker in a farming-connected sector, a politician, an agricultural bureaucrat, or a member or employee of JA. Third, an individual-level analysis is consistent with many approaches across economics, political economy, and political science, and thus offers common analytical ground between the disciplines.

The theoretical model is illustrated in Figure 4-1. It holds that (1) ideas arise within a specific historical and cultural context; (2) ideas shape values, which may include both economic and non-economic values; and (3) values shape policy preferences among the public and policymakers. Policy preferences are assumed to influence policy outcomes, though the transmission mechanism and possible distortions in aggregation and policy implementation are not detailed in the current model. Ideas, values, preferences, and policies are assumed in turn to influence history and culture in continuous iterative processes.

FIG. 4-1: A MODEL OF HOW IDEAS SHAPE VALUES, PREFERENCES, AND POLICIES

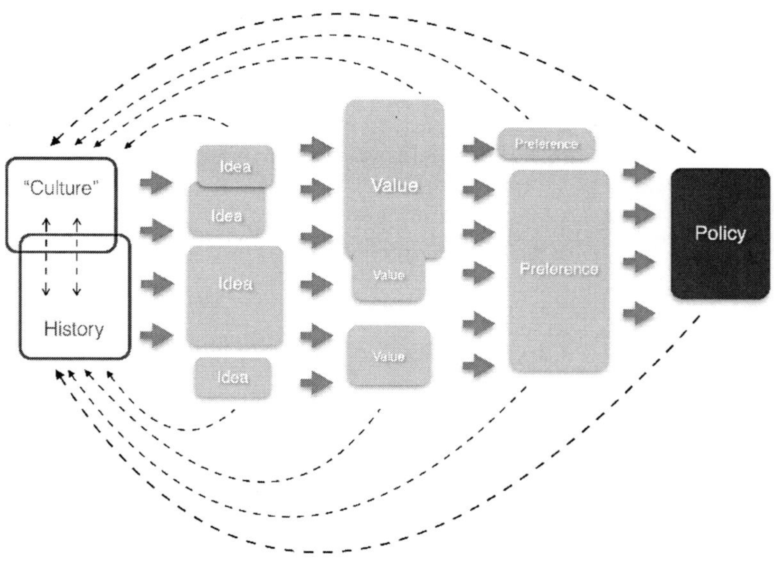

The first stage of the model includes culture and history. Culture here is defined after North (2006, 1006) as "the accumulated beliefs and inherited institutions from the past that provide the framework within which we begin thinking about problems." History refers to those past events that have happened in or to a society and that have some status in collective memory. Together, culture and history reflect the prior experiences and customs of a society as they have been transmitted and are understood in a contemporary context. The arrows linking history and culture to the next stage of the model represent the vectors by which they are transmitted. This would include intergenerational interactions, formal education systems, books, newspapers, and other forms of mass media.[49]

The second stage is ideas. In this approach, we take ideas to mean 'causal beliefs' and 'guides for action', after Béland and Cox (2011), and 'mental constructs,' after Skogstad (1998). Ideas operate as mental constructs within the mind of each individual to suggest either causal connections about the how the world *does* work or normative connections about how the world *should* be. In epistemological terms, we prefer a constituent logic, namely that ideas provide the conditions to *shape* policy preferences, rather than to determine them mechanistically. Stated another way, this is not an argument for historical or cultural determinism, but one that allows cultural and historical factors to play a role in shaping ideas, values, and preferences. Ontologically, we incline towards analytical duality, meaning that the distinction between material factors and ideas occurs in the mind rather than that distinction being an external and predetermined reality. That is to say, while material *objects* certainly have an existence outside of an individual, material *interests* can only be understood through an individual's cognitive faculties, making it appropriate to analyse material interests as a subset of ideas. However, the applicability of the model does not require the adoption of either of these philosophical positions.

Any society will typically include a broad range of ideas, and the range of ideas with contemporary currency will vary over time, although it follows logically that ideas that are more deeply embedded in the cultural and historical context of a society are more likely to endure, barring some event that discredits them. Where a related set of ideas gains broad acceptance and comes to form the lens through which political and economic issues are analysed, those ideas may form a policy paradigm in the sense articulated by Hall (1993). The vector arrows at this stage include newspapers and other mass media, books, political speech, and other such forms of transmitting ideas.

Ideas are not taken to shape preferences directly but rather do so through an intermediate third stage: values. Here, the model draws on a constructivist approach in international relations theory, Kuniko Ashizawa's account of a "value-action framework," developed to examine the role of state identity in determining foreign policy choices.[50] According to Ashizawa (2008), two elements of orthodox philosophical theories of actions equate to the political science term 'value', namely "pro-attitudes towards actions of a certain kind" and "beliefs that an action is of that kind." Due to "value complexity," multiple values may exist, and some of these may be mutually incompatible. Thus, multiple values are processed by an individual to produce one or more "dominant value(s)," which then shape preferences towards policies that are perceived to reflect that value. Here, the vector arrows linking preferences to the next stage represent internal mental processes.

At the fourth stage is policy preferences, our dependent variable. 'Preference' is defined after Ashizawa (2008, 579) as a type of intention towards a desired state of affairs that is involved in the pursuit of a particular action. Preferences may be expressed explicitly, as evidenced through opinion surveys, lobbying activities, or political speech, or inferred indirectly such as through electoral voting behaviour. The vector arrows linking values to the next stage represent the mechanisms by which preferences are translated into policies.

At the fifth stage of the model is policy, as implemented by the government. In democratic societies, the mechanisms by which preferences shape policies include elections, lobbying, and other indirect means by which popular opinions influence policymakers. While it is recognised that various factors impact the aggregation of voter preferences in the formation of policy,[51] it is assumed that in democratic systems the policies adopted to some greater or lesser extent reflect the preferences of the electorate. For example, in a study of the influence of Japanese public opinion on foreign policy, Midford (2011) found evidence that public opinion had a powerful impact on policy outcomes.

Thus, unlike approaches that treat ideas like a 'black box', this model offers a clear account of where ideas arise from, i.e, from within the cultural and historical context of a given society. It also makes explicit the fact that multiple values and policy preferences can and do exist for individuals. This *value complexity* is in keeping with the Hausman-McPherson framework in Table 3-1, where welfare, freedom, rights, and justice were all noted as types of outcomes that could be valued by individuals. The fact that a variety of factors influence ideas, values, and preferences also creates a natural connection with other scholarly disciplines outside of political economy, and allows for the incorporation of relevant data and insights from history, philosophy, cultural anthropology, and other academic fields, which can further strengthen the analysis.

There is also no requirement that the values held by an individual be logically consistent with each other, nor that they remain unchanging over time. Rather, as the dotted outer arrows indicate, there is an ongoing and multidirectional flow between culture, history, ideas, values, preferences, and policies, allowing for the fact that ideas, values, and preferences inevitably change and develop for both societies and individuals.

Finally, while the model is designed to have broad applicability, for the purposes of this study it will be used to analyse the following ideational variables in terms of how they shape agricultural policy preferences in Japan, as outlined previously in Chapter 1:

(1) ideas about agriculture as a normal part of the economy and business;
(2) ideas about agriculture as having a significant role in Japan's history and culture;
(3) ideas about agriculture related to societal welfare, such as income equality;
(4) ideas about agriculture related to national security, such as food self-sufficiency;
(5) ideas about agriculture related to health and food safety;
(6) ideas about agriculture related to the environment; and
(7) ideas about agriculture related to other reasons that are non-economic in nature, in the sense of not being primarily linked to economic concerns.

******

This chapter has examined the treatment of ideas in related approaches in political science, and developed an original model for how ideas can shape policy preferences, with reference to the links between culture, history, ideas, values, preferences, and policy. The next three chapters apply this approach to the study of agrarian ideas in Japan as follows.

Chapter 5 investigates the origins of ideas in terms of culture and history, through an examination of agrarian thought in early-modern and modern Japan, with a focus on the *nōhonshugi* tradition of agrarian fundamentalism. Chapter 6 examines the articulation and development of ideas in modern policy debates in the latter part of the twentieth century, through a content analysis of how agriculture was framed in newspaper editorials concerning the 1961 and 1999 agricultural basic laws. Chapter 7 then studies the values and preferences of individuals through survey data of attitudes towards agriculture and agricultural policy from the 1970s until today.

CHAPTER 5

"AGRICULTURE IS THE FOUNDATION OF THE NATION": AGRARIAN THOUGHT UNTIL THE 1930S

What kinds of ideas about agriculture were expressed in early modern and modern Japan? What are the origins of these ideas, and how did they develop? And how did ideas about agriculture vary between the ruling classes and popular thinkers? This chapter answers these questions by analysing the writings of important figures in agrarian thought from the seventeenth century until the first half of the twentieth century. It first surveys the most notable and influential ideas to illustrate the breadth and complexity of thought concerning agriculture and its roles in relation to society and the individual, and then develops an original typology of agrarian ideas to illustrate their occurrence over time. Building on the theoretical model outlined above, this chapter ultimately offers a deeper historical and cultural context for the ideas that subsequently appeared in agricultural policy debates in postwar and contemporary Japan.

The agrarian ideas discussed can all be connected to the diverse body of thought known as *nōhonshugi*, which arose in the nineteenth century and remained prominent until the 1930s. Nōhonshugi has been translated variously as "agriculture-is-the-base-ism" (Ogura, 1980 1; Waswo, 1989, 555), "agriculture-as-the-essence-ism" (Havens, 1974, 7), 'the doctrine of agriculture as the foundation,' or most simply 'agrarian fundamentalism'. Proponents, in turn, were known as *nōhonshugisha*. While details varied from thinker to thinker, the basic tenets of nōhonshugi often included a concern with the agricultural economy, an emphasis on rural communalism, and a belief that farming was inherently linked to the qualities or national essence that made Japan unique (Havens, 1974, 8).

Adherents of traditional or bureaucratic strands of nōhonshugi typically envisioned an economic and sometimes spiritual revival within existing social structures, while many advocates of popular variants of nōhonshugi desired a spiritual revival often involving social change, and also used real or imagined agrarian communities of the past as a site from which to critique the unfolding modernity of their day and offer an alternative model for contemporary society. In the 1930s, certain popular nōhonshugisha became increasingly associated with the political violence of ultranationalism, such that agrarian fundamentalism as a strand of political thought became largely discredited in postwar Japan. Despite this troubled dénouement, nōhonshugi remains a valuable window into influential ideas about the historical and modern roles of agriculture in Japanese society, while elements of this body of thought can still be found in public debates in the present day.

This chapter considers Tokugawa-era ideas and thinkers who were precursors for later views, bureaucratic agrarianism in the Meiji period, and the popular agrarianism of leading proponents in the early twentieth century. It then offers a typology of ideas, summarising each thinker's major contribution and areas of emphasis, to chart the development of agrarian ideas over time. English translations are quoted as they appear in the cited works.

5.1 Early Modern Thought: from Banzan to Ninomiya

The ideology of the Tokugawa system (circa 1600-1868) in early modern Japan drew heavily on Chinese political ideas, in particular those of Confucius, and the aim of the Tokugawa rulers was to create "a society in which everyone had their place and their duties and responsibilities to those above and below them" (Francks, 1999, 21). In the view of Kenneth Pyle (1998, 137), "Tokugawa political thought regarded agriculture as the basis of society." However, Stephen Vlastos (1998, 80) has argued that the valorisation of farming as being at the heart of the Japanese nation, although having some roots in Tokugawa nativist thought, was in fact a later construct in reaction to the societal changes and anxieties arising from modernisation. While many writers in this period mentioned agriculture in their work, among the most noteworthy writings on the topic were by Kumazawa Banzan, Ogyū Sorai, Andō Shōeki, Satō Nobuhiro, and Ninomiya Sontoku.

Farmer-soldiers

In the economic philosophy of Kumazawa Banzan (1619-91), agriculture was at the heart of the economy. Banzan[52] was a scholar and government administrator in the Okayama domain of western Japan, whose Confucianism-based writings and attempts at reforms brought him to prominence. Prefiguring the more developed economic theory of the French Physiocrats of the following century, he saw agriculture as the source of all wealth, and advocated for a grain-based economy with rice rather than precious metals as the medium of exchange, as encapsulated in the phrase *kikoku senkin*—'revere grain, despise gold'. Banzan also understood that the samurai class was in essence parasitic on the farming class, and proposed returning to an imagined model from former times when samurai lived as farmer-soldiers (*nōhei*) (Morris-Suzuki, 1989, 14-18).

Root and branches

Ogyū Sorai (1666-1728), perhaps the leading neo-Confucian philosopher of the era, shared a similar economic view to Banzan, seeing agriculture as the basis of society. Sorai articulated a standard Confucian position towards agriculture: "[t]o take care of the roots and to keep the branch under control; this is the principle taught by the sages of old. The root is agriculture, the branches, industry and commerce" (Pyle, 1998, 137). In addition to a hereditary class system and a stable social order, Sorai believed that a sound agrarian economy was essential for proper government, and that samurai would become physically stronger (and their women more frugal) if they moved out from the cities and onto the land as farmer-soldiers (de Bary et al, 2010).

Technological improvements and political importance

If Banzan and Sorai represented a bureaucratic strand of agricultural thought, Andō Shōeki (1703-62) and Satō Nobuhiro (1769-1850) contributed more to popular and practical ideas on farming, emphasising that yields could be improved through technological improvements and education rather than Confucian frugality and diligence (Havens, 1974, 23). They also shared a view of agriculture as a fundamental or special sphere. Andō, a medical doctor, agrarian philosopher, and idealist, "valued the natural act of direct cultivation of the land and stressed the mutuality of such an act" (Tsuzuki, 2005, 25).

In a plan for total government by Satō Nobuhiro,[53] the foremost of six government departments outlined was the "Ministry of Fundamental Affairs," with 'fundamental affairs' referring to agriculture (de Bary et al, 2010). Satō viewed the "peasantry" as "the base of the State" and agriculture as "the source of politics" (Ogura, 1980, 2). However, Satō's preference for centralised government was in contrast to the later advocacy of village communalism and localism by populist agrarian thinkers.

Farming and virtue

The teachings of Ninomiya Sontoku[54] (1787-1856) represented the high-point of popular agrarianism in the Tokugawa period (Havens, 1974, 25). A successful farmer and leader of rural development, Ninomiya taught that the "Way of Heaven and Nature" and the "Way of Humankind" should be connected, and that people must be accepting of the vagaries of nature and make their plans accordingly, rather than trying to act against the conditions set by nature (de Bary et al, 2010). His teachings centred on the idea of *hōtoku*, meaning 'repaying virtue'—that benefits received from heaven, nature, and society should be repaid, such as by accumulating savings through frugality and loaning these funds without interest to other farmers in the local village to finance structural improvements. The virtues necessary for achieving hōtoku included sincerity, diligence, thrift, and yielding to others (Havens, 1974, 25-26).

Ninomiya's teachings subsequently became the basis of the Hōtoku movement (*hōtokukai*), which began in the Meiji era and received official endorsement in 1906 when the Home Ministry established a Central Hōtokukai with branch offices throughout the country (Waswo, 1989, 573). The Hōtokukai practiced a form of mutual support including a credit union, teaching interconnectedness and a belief that the unaided sufferings of some members in times of distress would come to affect and hold back entire communities (de Bary et al, 2010). In the words of the twentieth-century Hōtokukai leader Fukuzumi Masae, "[m]en who wish to render thanks to Heaven by benefitting mankind as much as they can; men who wish to reform villages in order to help the poor; men who wish to sow the seeds of goodness that they may enjoy its lovely flowers and noble fruit; of such men does the 'Hōtokukai' exist" (de Bary et al, 2010).

During the Tokugawa period, the shogunate "lionized" farming in word if not in practice, for a range of reasons, including to reflect a Confucian ideological view of society, to maximise its own revenues from farming, and to stabilise society (Havens, 1974, 21). Indeed, Havens viewed the portrayal of agriculture as the root of society with trade and industry as the branches as an "arid but time-honoured maxim" that had been "a canon of state economic policy for many centuries in Japan" (1974, 20). However, by the mid-nineteenth century, the "orthodox notion of the static, rice-based economy had fallen into increasing disrepute" (Suzuki-Morris, 1989, 43). Following the forced opening of the country to international trade (termed *kaikoku*) and the modernisation programme that followed the Meiji Restoration, various nōhonshugisha would reach back to the ideas of individuals like Banzan, Sorai, and Ninomiya as they sought to construct a vision of agriculture for their own society at a time of rapid and fundamental change.

5.2 Bureaucratic Agrarianism from the Meiji Era onward

The immediate context for the bureaucratic agrarianism that arose in the Meiji era was the agricultural reform programme enacted in the first decades after the Restoration. Moving away from the 'root and branch' view and towards the economic liberalism popular in Europe, many leaders of the Meiji Restoration rejected the idea that farming had special social importance, and instead treated it like other industries and promoted capitalism in the countryside (Vlastos, 1998, 81). Farmers were for the first time granted legal rights to their land under the land tax reform of 1873, but also required to pay a monetary tax rather than an in-kind tax as before (Crawcour, 1989, 608).

The new political leaders sought to spread new techniques, technologies, and education, and implement structural improvements to improve crop production (Mosk, 2008, 109; Sugihara, 1996, 156). A farm promotion agency was set up in the 1870s, which became part of the new Ministry of Agriculture and Commerce (*Nōshōmushō*), established in 1880 and reorganised in 1885. Farm scale became a major issue of policy debate, with competing positions advocating large-scale farming (*dainō-ron*), medium-scale farming (*chūnō-ron*), and small-scale farming or 'peasantism' (*shōnō-ron*). Home Minister Ōkubo Toshimichi (1830-78), agriculture minister Inoue Kaoru (1836-1915), and other Restoration leaders were advocates of introducing large-scale production, but attempts to implement such measures in Hokkaido and elsewhere largely ended in failure (Ogura, 2000, 109), as did the introduction of foreign plants and animals ill-suited to Japan's soil and climate (Sugihara, 1996, 155).

Even if the overall thrust of economic policy favoured industry, some early Meiji leaders continued to speak of agriculture in terms that echoed the discourse of the Tokugawa era. Ōkubo, when director of the Land Tax Revision bureau, wrote that "[s]ince my country is founded on agriculture, when the peasantry can nurture energy and be engaged in their activities, the population would become stable" (Ogura, 1980, 11). Matsukata Masayoshi, who presided as finance minister over an era of deflation that hurt many farmers (detailed below), wrote that, "the State should be based on agriculture. When agriculture does not thrive, even if commerce and manufacture flourish, the State will not be secure" (Ogura, 1980, 16). Even the Emperor Meiji himself, on the occasion of opening the Komaba Agricultural School (later part of Tokyo University) in 1878, said in a speech that, "We consider agriculture the base of the State. Through it, production increases, and the people become wealthy. This is why agricultural sciences should be studied" (Ogura, 1980, 11, 16).

Towards the turn of the century, a generation of bureaucrats with concern for the problems of villages sought to help small-scale farms and village landowners alike, in order to improve production and counter the negative impact of industrialisation on the countryside (Havens, 1974, 57), an outlook that came to be termed bureaucratic nōhonshugi. Vlastos (1998, 80) suggests that this "elitist and conservative" variant of nōhonshugi became the dominant form, and that it warned that "the one-sided development of industry and a neglect of agriculture undermined society's natural bulwark against social revolution." That is to say, rural areas were viewed as an essential conservative counterpoint to socially progressive cities. Early bureaucratic agrarianists included Ishikawa Rikinosuke and Maeda Masana. Shinagawa Yajirō, Tani Kanjō, and Yokoi Tokiyoshi articulated notable views in the 1890s and 1900s, while later figures included Ishiguro Tadaatsu.

Practicality and morality

Ishikawa Rikinosuke (1845-1915) was a successful small-scale farmer from Akita who spent time working in the local bureaucracy. He became known for promoting the idea of *tekisanchō* ('appropriate production investigation'), a method of village self-help that emphasised technical aspects, education, and morality. The main point was "not simply to check the soil qualities of the fields and paddies. Rather it is to create talented men. If we do not nurture talented men, it will not matter how much profit or economy we have. These talented men must have honourable feelings towards Mother Nature" (Havens, 1974, 59).

Another prominent farmer and administrator, Maeda Masana (1850-1921), conducted a research tour in Europe and then surveyed the Japanese countryside in the 1880s (Crawcour, 1989, 414). He is notable for his work as chief editor of *Kōgyō Iken* (Advice on Promoting Enterprise), a thirty-volume study published in 1884 that subsequently became the basis for the government's agricultural policy. Maeda emphasised the need for more capital in agriculture, which could be provided through government loans, as well as agricultural societies, new technologies, and experimentation centres. Although he also advocated farmers showing more forbearance and diligence, his approach was less moralistic than that of Ishikawa (Havens, 1974, 61). Maeda believed that agricultural policy should be based on an intimate knowledge of the practical circumstances of farmers, and his detailed survey became the basis for future official surveys (Ogura, 1980).

Agricultural protection and self-rule

Shinagawa Yajirō (1843-1900), a student of the influential intellectual Yoshida Shōin who became a leading bureaucrat and later minister of internal affairs from 1891, was one of the most important agrarian voices of this period. At odds with the industrial promotion policies advocated by many other government leaders, he offered a pro-farming view that again emphasised the foundational role of agriculture for the family and the state:

> Agriculture is the foundation of the family and the foundation of the country. First came the fields, then families and villages, and then the country began... This agriculture must be called the basis of all occupations and the foundation of the state. Japan originally used agriculture to establish a state, and all such things as public taxes and families' food and clothing came from the land. All sorts of institutions were also based on farming. This may be called a true agriculture-based country.
>
> (Quoted in Havens, 1974, 65)

Shinagawa was notable for contributing to at least two developments in bureaucratic agrarian thought (Havens, 1974, 68-9). First, he stressed the need to protect farming against the spread of the commercial economy so that it could continue contributing to national economic development. Second, he argued that society should be based on elements of self-rule and the spirit of village communalism. Shinagawa's approach in these respects had similarities with that of Count Hirata Tōsuke, architect of the Industrial Cooperatives Law (*Sangyō Kumiaihō*) of 1899-1900, a bureaucratic initiative to aid impoverished agricultural producers (Pyle, 1998, 138-9).

National security and food self-sufficiency

General Tani Kanjō[55] (1837-1911) was a soldier and statesman from Kōchi prefecture on Shikoku island who opposed imperialism, served as the first Minister for Agriculture and Commerce, and defended farming on national security grounds. He linked agriculture with nationalism, was described as "the first advocate" of the ideas of food self-sufficiency, and was also a proponent of agricultural protection (Ogura, 1980, 35). In an 1898 speech Tani opined that, "[o]ften in modern military societies there is talk of self-sufficiency in ordnance… Even more than self-sufficiency in ordnance, we need self-sufficiency in foodstuffs" (Havens, 1974, 76). Tani echoed the idea of the farmer-soldier and suggested that the foundation of the state would be in danger if the numbers of farmers declined. He believed that Japan needed a secure body of socially conservative farmers as a barrier to radical thought and to supply healthy soldiers, as well as for food production (Pyle, 1998, 137). These views were shared by other soldier-statesmen like Count Hirata, who also served as agriculture minister from 1901 to 1903. Tani's views of agriculture's contribution to food production and the peasantry's contribution to social stability gave rise to his view on protection. Agriculture had fallen behind industry, he thought, and therefore needed to be encouraged and supported "by all means" (Ogura, 1980, 34).

Despite the sympathies of certain senior officials like Tani and Hirata, government policies in the Meiji era often made life difficult for small cultivator-farmers (*jisakunō*). During the Matsukata deflation of 1881-85 when the government pursued fiscal retrenchment and a tight monetary policy, farmers faced falling nominal prices but fixed monetary land taxes, and many had to sell their title deeds and become tenants on their own land, resulting in tenancy rates rising to around 45% by the early 1900s (Mosk, 2008, 103). In the 1890s and 1900s, policies increasingly favoured large landlords. For example, the *sangyō kumiai* producers' cooperatives had ostensibly been created to improve farmers' living standards and productivity, but in fact soon came to be dominated by landlords (Bullock, 1997). This policy disconnect would contribute to the growth of more populist forms of agrarian thinking in the subsequent decades.

Social stability

Yokoi Tokiyoshi (1860-1927) built on the innovations of Shinagawa and Tani to help transform agrarian thought from progressive and growth-oriented to a backward-looking defence against the advance of capitalism, based on his view of farming as the social, military, and ethical foundation of Japan (Havens, 1974, 98). An agricultural administrator and bureaucrat and later professor at Tokyo Agricultural University, Yokoi is believed to have coined the term *nōhonshugi* in 1897 in an essay that argued that the Way of Agriculture (*nōgyōdō*) was the successor to the Way of the Warrior (*bushidō*) (Gluck, 1987, 180). On the concept of *nōhei*, Yokoi thought that farmers were best suited to be soldiers in physical and moral terms, yet he feared that the increasing gap with the urban rich was enervating farmers and could result in socialism and violent upheaval, as had happened in Europe (Vlastos, 1998, 83).

Yokoi's philosophy continued to develop, and in his 1927 work *Shōnō ni kan suru kenkyū* ('Studies Concerning Small-scale Farming'), Yokoi outlined a more radical agrarian theory explaining why small-scale farming was different from large-scale farming. Whereas large-scale farming was a capitalist enterprise driven by the desire to produce marketable goods for profit, Yokoi believed that the small-scale farming typical in Japan operated under a different logic: maximising the utilisation of household labour (Vlastos, 1998, 86). The small farmer "willingly puts out the maximum labor, takes pleasure in work, and is in sympathy with the environment, and finds happiness nurturing the growth of plants and animals," he thought (quoted in Vlastos, 1998, 86). Villages in which everyone was motivated by this labour utilisation principle would live in harmony, whereas the absence of this would break down cohesion and give rise to capitalist forms of farming.

Though the government had assumed a laissez-faire approach to the countryside in the 1910s and 1920s, in light of mounting rural distress, the state once again took on an interventionist role toward agriculture after the onset of the Great Depression. A leading bureaucratic agrarianist in this period was Ishiguro Tadaatsu (1884-1960), vice-minister for agriculture and forestry in the 1930s and minister from 1940 until 1945. Ishiguro was a strong admirer of Ninomiya Sontoku, and later in life financed an English translation of his work (Ogura, 1980, 6). Ishiguro reaffirmed the view that the essence of farming was not commercial, but he also recognised the economic reality of the day:

> I believe that properly speaking the essence of agriculture is noncommercial. But commercial is what farm households that are being established under current conditions are becoming. I do not mean that there should be no contact at all with [commercialism]. To live today it is necessary for people to obtain money. But making money means manufacturing and selling things

> in order to buy other things, and this is not the essence of farmers' livelihoods. When you come into contact with a money economy, money gradually becomes more and more necessary, and you become commercial. Finally, some people come to believe that making money is the farmer's ideal.
>
> (quoted in Havens, 1974, 151)

Later, as minister, Ishiguro re-articulated a Confucian view of agriculture in the context of an industrialised modern economy:

> In our country the words "agriculture is the foundation of the nation" have virtually become the racial faith of the Yamato people. During the era of free enterprise we have been most oblivious of the point that agriculture must be respected, and it has been easy to scorn it. During my nearly thirty years as an agriculture and forestry official, I have always done my best to battle the emphasis on free enterprise capital… To say that "agriculture is the foundation of the nation" is never to stress merely the benefits of agriculture alone. Our ideal, from both the point of view of Nōhonshugi and that of the world at large, is not such a selfish way of thinking. Because it is the foundation of the country, we respect agriculture. Agriculture which is not the foundation of the country has no value whatever.
>
> (quoted in Havens, 1974, 151)

At its essence, bureaucratic agrarianism could be characterised as sympathetic paternalism underpinned by the belief that owner-cultivator farmers were more socially conservative and hence provided a bulwark against revolutionary ideas in a rapidly changing and volatile period for society. From the advent of the Meiji era through to the 1930s, bureaucratic thinkers shifted from a focus on technological improvement with some moral exhortations of farmers, towards a view of the inherent value of farming and the multiple benefits it brought the nation, even as the sector suffered from the effects of urban industrialisation and rural economic depression. This latter view also found popular expression in the 1920s and 1930s in a more radical romantic popular agrarianism.

5.3 Popular Agrarianism in the Early Twentieth Century

The agricultural sector had suffered another severe downturn from 1920 as the high food demand of the war years 1914 to 1918 came to an end and prices collapsed, yet the government's *laissez-faire* approach to agriculture in the 1910s continued during the following decade. Farmers in the 1920s were beset by bad harvests and high taxes (Freiner, 2019, 3), and the growing sense of rural crisis was compounded by the deflationary policies pursued by the government and the collapse of silk prices after the 1929 global crash, which destroyed the previously profitable and export-competitive sericulture industry.

The response of farmers to these circumstances was two-fold: tenancy disputes, and the emergence of a popular agrarianism that had socially revolutionary overtones.[56] Large landowners, especially in the Tōhoku region, began espousing a traditional form of agrarianism based on spiritual regeneration within existing social structures (Waswo, 1989, 589), in the same vein as bureaucratic agrarianists. At the same time, among farmers and populist thinkers, a more radical variant of agrarianism gained ground.

This new popular strand of nōhonshugi combined idealised views of historical village communalism and a strong sense of patriotic loyalty to the emperor (rather than to the contemporary state) with a critique of modern capitalism and the cities—and often of Western rationalism too. Indeed, Vlastos considered it a "two-voiced discourse" from "angry outsiders," one voice a "furious, apocalyptic polemic against industrial capitalism and urban culture," the other a "utopian discourse on rural harmony and social cohesion," with a conservative affirmation of existing property relations and the farm family at its core (1998, 80). The two leading thinkers of this radical romantic agrarian nationalism were Gondō Seikyō and Tachibana Kōzaburō.

Village self-rule

Gondō Seikyō[57] (1868-1937) was born to a small owner-cultivator farm family in Fukuoka prefecture. In early life he was associated with the ultranationalist Amur River Society that pressed for Japan's imperialist expansion in Korea and China, and despite little formal schooling he later became a private academy lecturer and leader of several study societies in Tokyo. Gondō felt that the "common people" of Japan had fallen on "evil days," and blamed for their plight the military-centred "plutocracy," closely linked to the bureaucracy and the *zaibatsu* business conglomerates; in his view, the people were "pursued by cold and hunger, and unless they work in the midst of their tears as tools of the plutocrats and those holding political power, they cannot stay alive" (de Bary et al, 2010). For Gondō, the solution for the nation's contemporary problems lay in its past.

Gondō's central idea was that of *self-rule* in the context of agricultural villages. He believed that Japanese life had historically been based on small communities, and that a return to agricultural villages would allow for autonomous living. Like other Asian countries, Japanese society had been founded on agricultural cultivation by peasants rather than on animal domestication by herders as in the West, he contended. Agricultural work and community ties were thus both traditional and essential in Japanese society, and were also required as a way for people to give thanks to the gods for the blessings of nature (Najita and Harootunian, 1998, 219-20). The emperor had an essential role as the sacred symbol of the national community, but the centralised government and the army were to be distrusted both because they broke the historical tradition of village communalism, and also because in their concern only with industrial production they had become separated from the sacred agrarian foundations of Japanese civilisation (Najita and Harootunian, 1998, 219-20). Japan, in Gondō's view, needed to return to village communalism and self-rule:

> Self-rule arose gradually and naturally. It developed as food, clothing, and shelter were taken care of. It is harmonised by the true values of coexistence and mutual prosperity. But the institutions of our country throughout the centuries have not yet attained this. The ravages of nature and the biases of the authorities have blocked the progress of self-rule. There is a general trend toward ruin and outbreak of evils, [evident from] the divergence between those who work and those who are idle, the estrangement between the rich and the poor… Self-rule is the authority over our lives. It is an article of faith for peace. It is the origin of human progress. It is the foundation for independence and self-strengthening.
>
> (quoted in Havens, 1974, 173)

Spiritual harmony and patriotic reform

Tachibana Kōzaburō[58] (1893-1974) shared with Gondō the view that the agrarian village community was the starting point of Asian civilisation and that the economic and political system adopted in the Meiji era needed to be replaced with one based around the link between the emperor and the people. In contrast to Gondō, he had a more negative view of village life in former times. As a youth, Tachibana had left an elite Tokyo high school to devote himself to work for rural regeneration in his Ibaragi hometown, establishing a successful family farming operation called *Kyōdai Mura* (Fraternal Village) and teaching his communal farming philosophy through the *Aikyōkai* (Community Loving Society) producers' cooperative and the *Aikyōjuku* academy.

At the heart of Tachibana's philosophy was the view that communal agricultural life allowed the individual to transcend the self and achieve spiritual fulfilment. Tachibana wrote that "[w]hen performed with a pure heart, diligent farm labour... spiritually and materially harmonises the interests of self and other" and "bestows the riches of true brotherhood," while working together in cooperation allowed people to understand "the true meaning of human existence and its attendant joys," filling them with virtue and securing their existence (Vlastos, 1998, 91). Aikyōkai members were sceptical both of the exploitative nature of feudal village life and of the top-down agricultural reforms of Meiji leaders devoted to building up the army and industry. One member of the group wrote that, since they were now conscious of their historical condition, the "time when farmers can be hoodwinked by such pure cant as 'Farmers are the Treasure of the Nation' is long gone" (Vlastos, 1998, 92;).

A second cornerstone of Tachibana's worldview was his opposition to modern capitalism and a related desire to overturn the current economic and political system through 'patriotic reform.' Capitalism had two particularly malevolent effects, he argued. The first was that the great cities like Tokyo knew nothing of the nation's land and farm villages and were "causing the ruin of the national land system that is a basic requirement for the existence of national society"; the second was the corrupting power of money, which had caused greed to supersede other values, commoditised everything (including dignity and integrity), and resulted in everything being "monopolised by the power of money" (Havens, 1974, 256-7).

The solution was to be found in "an imperial people's cooperative self-rule system based on patriotism and brotherhood... with the interests of all the people as its main point." There was to be some room for industry in this system but self-ruling communities would closely supervise business enterprises (with the assistance of a national parliament) for the good of the nation, and be united through a shared reverence for the symbolically (but not institutionally) important emperor, whom Tachibana valued in terms of his role as patron of agriculture and because of the purported origins of the monarchy in relation to the Shintō gods of rice planting and harvesting (Havens, 1974, 264-7).

The focus on the role of the family and traditional social relations as well as reverence for the emperor gave the Aikyōkai movement obvious shared ground with the political right. In the 1930s Tachibana embraced political violence as a strategy to achieve change in society, and many of the ultranationalists involved in the attempted coup d'état on May 15, 1932 were associated with both Tachibana and Gondō.

By this stage, nōhonshugi was synonymous with "the emergence of emperor-centred ultranationalism and Japanese fascism," having veered "from a pro-farming position… steadily towards antiurbanism and Japanese fascism" (Waswo, 1989, 555-6). Although their political legacy was understandably discredited in the postwar era of pacific liberal democracy, the agrarian philosophy of Gondō and Tachibana remains a notable articulation of the link between land, farmers, emperor, and state in Japan, drawing together both material and spiritual elements.

5.4 A Typology of Nōhonshugi Ideas

The diverse ideas located within the nōhonshugi body of thought ranged from idealistic notions of recreating harmonious agricultural villages from a mythical past through to concrete programs for increasing efficiency and productivity in order that farmers could contribute to a modern capitalist economy. This section develops an original typology of the range of ideas surveyed in this chapter, drawing on the categories of romantic agrarianism and rational agrarianism developed by the historian David Danbom in his study of agrarianism in the United States.

Romantic agrarianism emphasises the "moral, emotional, and spiritual benefits agriculture and rural life provides" to the individual (Danbom, 1991, 1). In the case of Japan, this must also include the benefits to society as a whole. Romantic agrarians tend to consider rural society to be inherently superior to urban society. The view can be traced to early Confucian philosophy in China, and was also expressed eloquently by the nineteenth century American writer Henry David Thoreau. In the twentieth century, romantic agrarianism also incorporated a strand of antimodernism, namely a critique of the social and economic changes caused by modern capitalist economic development.

Rational agrarianism, in comparison, stresses "the tangible contributions agriculture and rural people make to a nation's economic and political well-being" (Danbom, 1991, 1). Rational agrarians tend to accept the changes to agriculture resultant from economic development. They see a strong rural society as desirable for the practical benefits that it can bring to an economy, such as the provision of food and the productive employment of human and natural resources for the benefit of the entire country. Rational agrarianism considers how agriculture can contribute to the economy and how life for the rural population can be improved. The Physiocrats in France and Thomas Jefferson in the United States exemplified this variant of agrarianism in the eighteenth century.

A third category is also possible, one which doesn't put any special value on agriculture but instead advocates a market-based or laissez-faire approach that does not distinguish agriculture from other economic sectors. This is also the default position of modern economic analysis.

Table 5-1 shows the agrarian ideas or works associated with each of the prominent thinkers surveyed in this chapter and offers a classification of the orientation of their thought as romantic, rational, or market-based. It also gives some indication of the relative strength of expression of the three categories of ideas over time—whether it was a strong focus, a partial focus, or not a focus.

This classification suggests that romantic agrarianism was the primary concern of the majority of prominent thinkers during the period under consideration. In five cases, thinkers could be classified as primarily romantic agrarianists, while a further six combined rational and romantic elements of agrarian thought. Romantic agrarianism remained largely constant throughout the period among the thinkers surveyed here. Conversely, rational agrarianism, first appearing in the later eighteenth and early nineteenth centuries, became a strong concern in the early Meiji decades but declined in the economically and socially tumultuous years of the 1920s and 1930s. Of the individuals surveyed, only Ōkubo, Inoue, and Matsukata—important Restoration leaders but not typical nōhonshugisha—might be said to have a relatively market-oriented position, though other less influential individuals not surveyed here could also be included in this category.[59]

TABLE 5-1: TYPOLOGY OF NŌHONSHUGI THOUGHT IN JAPAN

Date	Thinker	Notable Idea or Work	Emphasis	Romantic	Rational	Market
mid 1600s	Banzan	Agriculture at the heart of the economy	Social, political, military	◉		
late 1600s, early 1700s	Sorai	'The root is agriculture, the branches industry and commerce'	Social, political, military	◉		
1700s	Andō	Technological improvements, importance of act of direct cultivation	Spiritual, technical	◉	•	
early 1800s	Satō	Agriculture as a 'fundamental affair' of state	Political		•	
early 1800s	Ninomiya	*hōtoku* (repaying virtue)	Moral, social	◉	•	
mid-1800s	Ōkubo	Large-scale production, introduction of new plants and animals	Economic, technical		•	◉
late 1800s	Inoue	Large-scale production	Economic			◉
late 1800s	Matsukata	Fiscal retrenchment, tight money	Economic		•	◉
late 1800s-early 1900s	Ishikawa	*tekisanchō* (appropriate production investigation)	Moral, economic	◉	◉	
late 1800s-early 1900s	Maeda	*Kōgyō Iken* (Advice on Promoting Enterprise)	Economic, technical	•	◉	

late 1800s	Shinagawa	Protect agriculture for economic development; self-rule and village communalism	Social, political	◉	◉
late 1800s	Hirata	Agricultural cooperatives	Social, political		◉
late 1800s-early 1900s	Tani	Self-sufficiency in foodstuffs, agricultural protectionism	Nationalism, national security, social, military		◉
late 1800s-early 1900s	Yokoi	Logics of farming and capitalism; farmer-nature relationship; agricultural protectionism	Moral, military	◉	
1920s-1930s	Ishiguro	Essence of farming is non-commercial	Social	◉	●
1920s-1930s	Gondō	Self rule in villages; village communalism	Social, political, moral	◉	
1920s-1930s	Tachibana	Act of farming harmonises self and other; 'patriotic' reform for self-rule system focused on emperor	Spiritual, social, political	◉	

Key: ◉=Strong focus; ●=partial focus

******

This chapter has provided a historical survey of ideas about agriculture, ranging from early articulations of agrarian thought from the Tokugawa period through the bureaucratic and popular variants of nōhonshugi from the Meiji era up to the 1930s. It also presents a typology of ideas, showing how romantic and rational strands of agrarianism developed over time, latterly coexisted with elements of market-based thinking about agriculture.

Leading Tokugawa thinkers saw agriculture as being at the centre of society and valued it as the source of all wealth, while the moral and spiritual aspects of cultivation were also considered important. Bureaucratic agrarianism in the Meiji period moved from paternalistic guidance to promote productivity, to valuing the social stability that rural villages provided and their contributions to national security through supplying food. Later bureaucratic agrarianists emphasised the inherent values of the act of farming, utilising Tokugawa-era thought in a critique of the spread of capitalism and the social changes that it caused. Popular agrarianists went further still, blaming the ills of rural communities on the military-bureaucratic-zaibatsu groups that dominated government. They also advocated a return to local self-rule and village communalism organised around a patriotic loyalty to the emperor as an alternative to the centralised capitalist state of the 1920s and 1930s. However, popular agrarianists turned increasingly towards political violence in the 1930s and became subsumed into the ultranationalist movement in that troubled decade, such that agrarian fundamentalism as a political viewpoint was delegitimised in the postwar era.

Irrespective of the historical veracity of certain elements or claims of the nōhonshugi view, what is of significance here is *how* agrarian thinkers and policy makers from the Tokugawa period onward conceptualised and portrayed agriculture and its position in relation to society and the state. In this respect, it seems clear that by the Meiji era, for many Japanese people agriculture was already considered as a special and distinct sphere. Agriculture was a part of the economy but was also considered to have been historically at the heart of society and the nation. On a practical level, rural villages supplied strong and healthy soldiers and farmers provided food for the nation, with farm protection advocated to ensure food self-sufficiency to strengthen national security. In moral terms, farmers were seen as having strong virtue, superior to urban residents motivated purely by profit. In spiritual terms, agriculture was deeply linked with the symbolic person of the emperor, whose priestly roles in the Shintō religion in turn included planting and harvesting rice and supplicating the rice-gods.

The data and analysis from this chapter operationalise the first stages of the theoretical framework outlined in Chapter 4 by examining historical and cultural factors and how they provide the context for specific ideas about agriculture. Some of these ideas have also had a feedback effect in that they shaped the later development of history and culture. This is most obvious in the case of the concept of overarching concept of nōhonshugi itself, which was grounded in perceptions of Japan's history and culture and which became an influential idea in the Meiji era and later. Other ideas identified as variables in Chapters 1 and 4 are also apparent in historical agrarian thought, including the societal aspect of maintaining farmers' incomes and agriculture's contribution to the nation's safety and security.

However, a link between historical and contemporary ideas in a society cannot simply be assumed, but rather needs to be demonstrated. From this background of historical ideas, the next chapter turns to ideas about agriculture in the second half of the twentieth century. Specifically, it examines the portrayal of agriculture in national newspaper editorial articles related to the agricultural basic laws enacted in 1961 and 1999, to study the framing of farming by the mass media in policy debates, and to trace the continuity and development of agrarian ideas during this period. It also serves to illustrate the role of the media as a vector of ideas.

CHAPTER 6

FRAMING FARMING: MEDIA PORTRAYALS IN THE BASIC LAW POLICY DEBATES

What ideas were important in public policy debates about agriculture in postwar Japan? Did economic or non-economic ideas predominate? And how did public policy debates about agriculture change over time? This chapter answers these questions by analysing the content of newspaper editorial articles during two crucial periods for agricultural policy in the postwar era— the debates around the framework-setting 1961 Agricultural Basic Law (*Nōgyō Kihon Hō*) and its replacement, the 1999 Food, Agriculture and Rural Areas Basic Law (*Shokuryō Nōgyō Nōson Kihon Hō*). It investigates the terms in which agriculture was framed during these debates, with particular focus on whether agriculture was portrayed either as a normal sector of the economy or in terms of issues not primarily related to its economic role, such as health and food safety, national security, societal wellbeing, and environmental protection.

6.1 The Basic Laws for Agriculture

The 1961 basic law was drawn up in response to the serious situation affecting the countryside by the later 1950s. The position of farmers had improved significantly during the initial years after World War II when the Supreme Commander for the Allied Powers (SCAP) administration transferred land ownership rights from landlords to tenant-farmers on terms that became very favourable due to the effects of hyperinflation subsequent to the setting of land sale prices. Ironically, it took an occupying force to finally implement the principle of owner-cultivators (*jisakunō chūshin shugi*) that had long been advocated by so many prewar agrarianists (Kosai, 1989, 496).[60] Farmers also benefitted from a major increase in government support for agriculture in 1949-53 as the Yoshida government sought to establish a stable conservative electoral base in rural constituencies (Calder, 1989, 257), and again from food demand to supply United Nations forces fighting in the Korean War (1950-53). From the mid-1950s, however, the situation deteriorated. Agricultural productivity fell relative to the manufacturing sector (Ogura, 1980), the government cut subsidies to farmers in the 1954-56 recession that followed the end of the Korean War, and then reduced the rice price in 1956-58 due to fiscal pressures (Calder, 1989, 234, 265). Rapid economic growth in cities drew the surplus agricultural labour workforce to urban areas at a rate of around 0.8% of the national population annually, with disruptive effects on rural society (see Figure 2-4).[61]

Often referred to in the media as the 'constitution for agriculture' (*nōgyō no kenpō*), the 1961 law provided the framework for agricultural policy until 1999. It was premised on addressing both the productivity gap and the income gap between agriculture and industry, two goals with a clear potential conflict. Specific aims included encouraging shifts in production to reflect the changing structure of food demand, and enlarging production unit sizes to foster "viable units" with household farm incomes comparable to non-farm households (Hayami, 1988, 48).

The 1999 basic law was also drawn up at a time of significant difficulty for the agricultural sector, with farmer numbers falling and the average farmer age and the total area of abandoned land both rising. One proximate cause of these difficulties was the agricultural liberalisation measures agreed as part of the 1994 Uruguay Round of the GATT/WTO, which saw the tariffication of non-tariff barriers and the implementation of minimum access requirements, including for rice. The ultimate causes, however, were surely the chronic decline in agriculture's productivity relative to industry, despite averaging 5.3% annual growth in 1960-80 (Hayami, 1988, 11), and a policy-induced failure to move away from rice production to more profitable crops during a period when consumption patterns diversified further towards Western foods and rice consumption declined steadily.

Agricultural policy after 1961 came to focus mainly on income support rather than productivity improvements, as exemplified by the gentan policy that paid farmers to limit rice production and set aside paddy fields from about 1970 onwards.[62] The assumption at the time of the first basic law was that the decreasing rural population would contribute to the consolidation of fragmented production (Fukui, 1975, 138). However, generous subsidies kept marginal farmers in business and mitigated against scale enlargements by more efficient farmers. As before, the 1999 law was premised on two potentially contradictory aims—in this case, the introduction of the market principle, and the development of sustainable agriculture.[63]

6.2 Media Analysis, Agenda-Setting, and Framing

The mass media play an important role in collating and diffusing information, opinions, and ideas in modern societies. Newspapers are one of the oldest mass media and, even in today's era of social media, still one of the most wide-reaching and respected. The value of examining newspaper editorials is at least two-fold. First, taken at face value, editorials may be understood as representing considered and concise expressions of the views of newspaper editorial writing committees, whose place in the hierarchy of nationally-connected news-gathering organisations offers the writers both overviews and unique insights into major policy issues. Seen this way, editorials are a useful source of informed opinions about agriculture and policy, containing information about the various practical and policy issues under discussion and their relative importance in public policy discourse.

Second, newspapers can also be analysed in terms of their role in agenda-setting. An agenda may be defined as "a set of issues that are communicated in a hierarchy of importance at a point in time" (Dearing and Rogers, 1996, 2). Within agenda-setting studies, three kinds of agendas are often analysed (Dearing and Rogers, 1996). The *media agenda* refers to the hierarchy of stories and issues presented by mass media, and may be measured by such techniques as a content analysis of the number and nature of news stories about a given topic. The *public agenda* refers to the hierarchy of concerns expressed by the general public, and is usually measured through opinion surveys. The *political agenda* refers to the hierarchy of concerns of politicians, government officials, and other policy actors, and can be measured by laws passed, budget allocations, or parliamentary debates.

Scholars of agenda-setting tend to assume that the media agenda influences the public agenda and that this in turn influences the political agenda (although the media agenda may also influence the political agenda directly), and that feedback loops exist. Thus, the media is held to have an important role in influencing both public debate and the political agenda. In the famous phrase of Bernard Cohen, the press "may not be successful much of the time telling people what to think, but it is stunningly successful in telling its readers what to think *about*" (quoted in Dearing and Rogers, 1996, 1).

Agenda-setting can be considered on two levels. First level agenda-setting refers to directing attention to certain *objects*, such as political candidates or political issues. With finite space, focusing on certain objects increases their *salience* relative to other objects. Second-level agenda-setting refers to the relative salience of particular *attributes* of an object (Weaver, 2007, 142). Attributes encompass "the entire rage of properties and traits that characterize an object" (McCombs, 2004, 70), and can range from simple, discrete facts like a candidate's age or gender through to complex, multi-faceted attributes, like the so-called 'War on Terror.'

The concept of *framing* refers to selecting and emphasising particular attributes for the media agenda when discussing an object, and can also be a way to organise news presentations and one's own thoughts about an object (McCombs, 2004, 87, 88). Frames can also be considered as "organizing principles incorporating and emphasizing certain lower level attributes to the exclusion of others" (McCombs, 2004, 88). The point of framing some attributes as more salient is "to promote a particular problem definition, causal interpretation, moral evaluation and/or treatment recommendation for the item described" (Entman, 1993, 52). Thus, to add to Cohen's maxim, the press may also tell us *how* to think about something, as well as what to think about—which comes rather close to telling us how to think (McCombs, 2004, 71).

6.3 Analysing Japanese Newspaper Editorials

Japanese people have been described as being "among the most eager readers of newspapers in the world" (Valaskivi, 2007, 28). Newspapers have had and continue to hold a prominent position in public life and policy discourse in Japan. The decline of newspaper readership in Japan in the internet era has been slower than in other countries, due in part to the strong readership tradition and the door-delivery system (Valaskivi, 2014, 65), and perhaps because newspapers were slow to develop their online presence, though readership decline has been accelerating from the mid-2010s. The four newspapers[64] included in this analysis represent a balanced range of opinion across the political spectrum.[65] Each publication is a well-established national newspaper in print for over 140 years, and each maintains daily sales of several million copies, making them among the highest-selling newspapers in the world.[66]

The *Yomiuri Shimbun*, founded in 1874, is the most politically conservative and right-leaning of the four newspapers. It is the largest-selling newspaper in Japan and among the largest-selling in the world as a whole. Daily sales in 2018 were around 8 million copies, down from 10 million in 2000. The *Asahi Shimbun*, founded in 1879, is the most politically liberal or left-leaning national newspaper in Japan. Its daily sales were around about 5.5 million in 2018, down from 8 million in 2000.[67] The *Mainichi Shimbun*, founded in 1872, is a moderately left-of-centre national newspaper. With daily sales of around 2.2 million in 2018, down from 4 million in 2000, it remains the third largest-selling newspaper in Japan. The *Nikkei Shimbun* (formally the *Nihon Keizai Shimbun*), founded in 1876, is a politically centrist and economically liberal newspaper focusing on economic and business news. Its daily sales were around 2.1 million in 2018, down from 3 million in 2000, making it the fourth largest-selling national newspaper.

The articles analysed below are all editorials on the topics of the 1961 Agricultural Basic Law or its 1999 replacement, the Food, Agriculture and Rural Areas Basic Law. The articles were identified via online searches of the digital archives of the four publications—the Asahi's *Kikuzo II Visual* archive, the Mainichi's *Maisaku*, the Nikkei's *Nikkei Telecom 21*, and the Yomiuri's *Yomidasu Rekishikan*. The keywords used for searches in both periods were the kanji characters for *nōgyō kihon hō* (agricultural basic law) and *shasetsu* (editorial). The time parameters for the searches were the four-year periods ending in the year of the enactment of the two laws in question: 1958-1961 for the Agricultural Basic Law, and 1996-1999 for the Food, Agriculture, and Rural Areas Basic Law. A total of 64 matching articles were identified, 16 for the 1961 period and 48 for the 1999 period.

The contents of the articles were analysed through a coding process to identify the ideas that were used to frame agriculture in each text. Through a process of iterative analysis, a set of ideational categories was identified and developed based on the occurrence of keywords related to that idea. For example, the words *kankyō* (environment), *osen* (pollution) and *seitai* (ecology) were collated in the framing category of 'environment.' In total, eleven ideational categories were identified: economy & business, society, environment, national security, culture & tradition, health & food safety, government intervention, market, multifunctionality, trade issue, and politics. Details of the categories are given in Table 6-1, and example sentences from the articles are provided in Appendix I.

TABLE 6-1 CODES, CATEGORIES, DEFINITIONS, AND KEYWORDS FOR FRAMING ANALYSIS

Code	Category/Frame	Definition	Keywords
01 ECB	Economic & Business	this frame portrays agriculture as being the same as other sectors in the economy, in terms of its role as a business enterprise for those engaged in it and its place as a 'normal' sector of the economy. This frame is consistent with orienting the agricultural sector along market-based lines.	efficiency, production, expansion, competitiveness, cost, scale, sector/industry, assets, investment, entrepreneur, consumer
02 SOC	Societal Wellbeing	portrays agriculture in terms of the wellbeing of society and groups of individuals that constitute it, with particular focus on those in challenging circumstances.	income equality/income gap, rural communities/farm villages, semi-mountainous (areas), women, elderly, sustainable, 'breadwinners' (*ninaite*), successor
03 ENV	Environment	portrays agriculture in terms of its role in maintaining the natural environment and ecosystems, such as fields, mountains, forests, waterways, and wildlife.	environment, pollution, ecology, wildlife, landslides/land disaster, (environmental and water) resources, fertilizer, agricultural chemicals, flood control, afforestation, national land

04 NSC	National Security	portrays agriculture in terms of its role in achieving aspects of national security, namely those issues which may be considered important for the survival of the nation and the state, like a secure national food supply.	food self-sufficiency, domestic reduction, stable supply, food security, stockpiling
05 CTN	Culture & Tradition	portrays agriculture in terms of its cultural, historical, and/or religious significance, and its role in contemporary society.	tradition, traditional, *washoku*, national diet
06 HFS	Health & Food Safety	portrays agriculture in terms of the contribution of agricultural products to health and nutrition, such as providing 'safe' food, food of high quality etc.	health, food safety, quality, nutrition
07 GOV	Government Intervention	portrays agriculture as an area in which government intervention to help or support farmers is appropriate, such as through financial support or other measures.	government/administration, income insurance, income compensation, subsidy, agricultural protection, official/government support, public works, *gentan*
08 MKT	Market	portrays agriculture as an appropriate area for utilizing or expanding market-oriented policies or a laissez-faire approach by the government.	market, market mechanism, liberalisation, market principle, supply, demand

09 MFN	Multifunctionality	portrays agriculture as having a multiplicity of functions in relation to the economy, society and especially the environment. By definition, this is a 'meta-frame' that incorporates several other frames, but it may be identified by name or by listing in close proximity a range of functions performed.	multifunctionality, roles of agriculture
10 TRD	Trade Issue	portrays agriculture in terms of its role as an issue in trade and international affairs such as imports, exports and trade agreement negotiations.	tariffs, tariffication, WTO, Uruguay Round, (trade) negotiations, internationalization (of the economy)
11 POL	Political Issue	portrays agriculture in terms of its importance as a domestic political issue, in relation to political parties and other major political actors.	pork-barrel, politicians, agricultural (tribe) politicians, election, politics, 'politically-coloured'

Having established the ideational categories, each article was coded by one of three ideational frames: dominant frame, secondary frame, or reference. *Dominant frame* referred to the single most significant ideational frame used to portray agriculture in the article. *Secondary frames* were frames that appeared with some degree of significance in the text as portrayals of agriculture but which were emphasised less than the dominant frames. Other, lesser mentions of a frame, in either a positive of negative sense, were recorded as *references*. In addition to the qualitative categorisation of the frames appearing in each article, each corpus of texts for 1961 and 1999 was also analysed quantitatively, in order to ascertain the numerical frequency of each category in terms of keywords, and then to show the most frequently occurring individual keywords across the two corpuses as a whole.

Finally, the eleven framing categories were meta-classified as being either economic or non-economic in nature. Economic here refers to a viewpoint attaching decisive or principal importance to economic goals or interests, equivalent to what the former MAFF vice-minister Ogura Takekazu termed 'economism' (Ogura, 1980). In this sense, three categories were considered to be economic in nature: *economic and business*, *market*, and *trade issue*. The other categories were considered to be non-economic in nature, in the sense that they are valued by individuals for achieving goals that are distinct from considerations of the economy, economic welfare, and GDP growth. The distinction is not absolute, in that all of the issues discussed could be considered to have economic dimensions.[68, 69]

6.4 Results of the 1961 and 1999 Analyses

Figure 6-1 shows the frequency of frames in articles relating to the 1961 Agricultural Basic Law. It is seen that a relatively small number of frames appeared in this set of editorials, with only 5 of the 11 framing classifications identified. Looking at the dominant frames, the most common was government intervention, with 6 occurrences. Economic & business was second with 4, and societal wellbeing had 3. Finally, market was the dominant frame in 2 articles and political issue in one. Among secondary frames, societal wellbeing was the most frequently occurring (12 occurrences), with economic & business having 10 and societal wellbeing 8. Political issue was a secondary frame in 3 editorial articles and market in two. When references were included in the results, a greater heterogeneity was observed, with 9 categories being recorded.

FIG. 6-1: EDITORIAL FRAMES FOR THE 1961 BASIC LAW

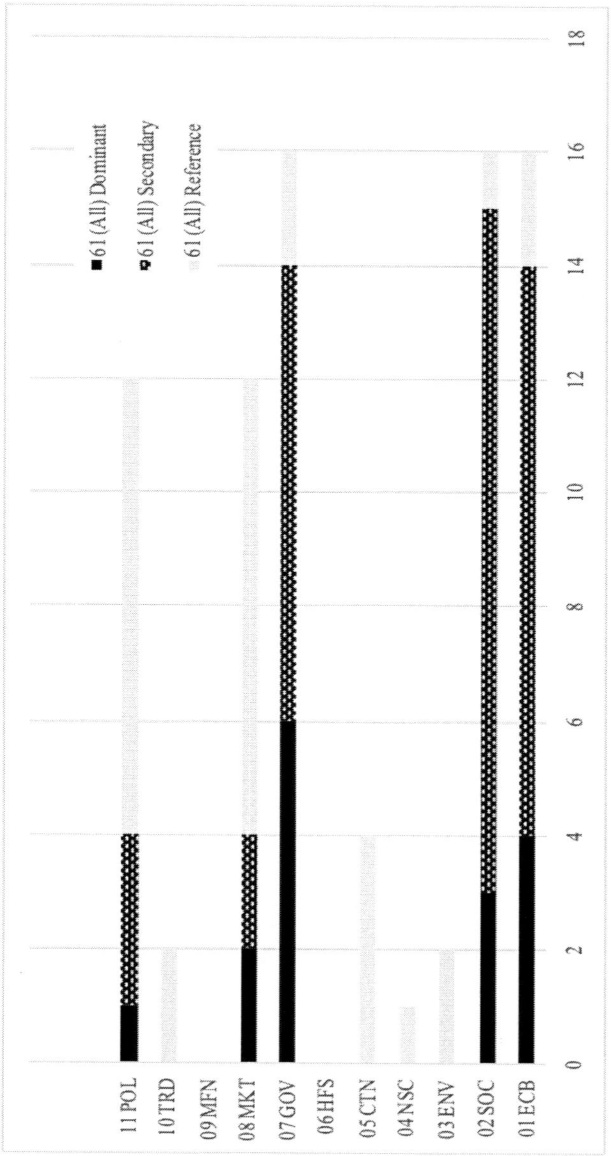

Considering the breakdown of these figures by newspapers, in the Asahi, societal wellbeing was the dominant frame in half of the articles, followed by economic & business, government intervention, and political issues. Among secondary frames, economic & business and government intervention were most common, followed by political issue and market. For the articles in the Yomiuri, government intervention was dominant in half of the articles, followed by economic & business and market. Looking at the secondary frames, societal wellbeing was the most numerous, followed by economic & business, government intervention, and market.

Turning to the 1999 Food, Agriculture, and Rural Areas Basic Law, Figure 6-2 shows the frequency of frames for the articles relating to this period. This set of articles exhibited a greater range than the earlier set, with all eleven framing categories identified at varying degrees of frequency. Looking at the dominant frames in all articles, economic & business was the most frequent, with 20 occurrences. Environment occurred 6 times, followed by trade (5), and national security and health & food safety (both 4). Societal wellbeing, market, and multifunctionality each occurred once. The range of secondary frames was even more varied. Societal wellbeing was the most common (22), followed by environment (19), national security and trade (both 17), economic & business (16), market and health & food safety (both 12), government intervention (11), multifunctionality (6) and culture & tradition (2). When references were included, the results were yet more diverse.

Considering the breakdown of the 1999 findings by newspaper, in the Asahi the most common dominant frame was the environment, followed by economic & business, and societal wellbeing. Among secondary frames, societal wellbeing was the most frequent, followed by environment, economic & business, health & food safety. In the Mainichi, the most common dominant frames were economic & business and national security, followed by government intervention, multifunctionality and trade issue. Among secondary frames, societal wellbeing was the most common, followed by economic & business and environment, trade, national security, government intervention and market.

In the Yomiuri, the most common dominant frame was economic & business, followed by trade issue. Among secondary frames, health & food safety was the most common, followed by trade, environment, and national security. In the Nikkei, the most common dominant frame was economic & business, followed by government intervention, and trade issue. Among secondary frames, national security, societal wellbeing, environment, economic & business and trade issue were most common in that order.

FIG. 6-2: EDITORIAL FRAMES FOR THE 1999 BASIC LAW

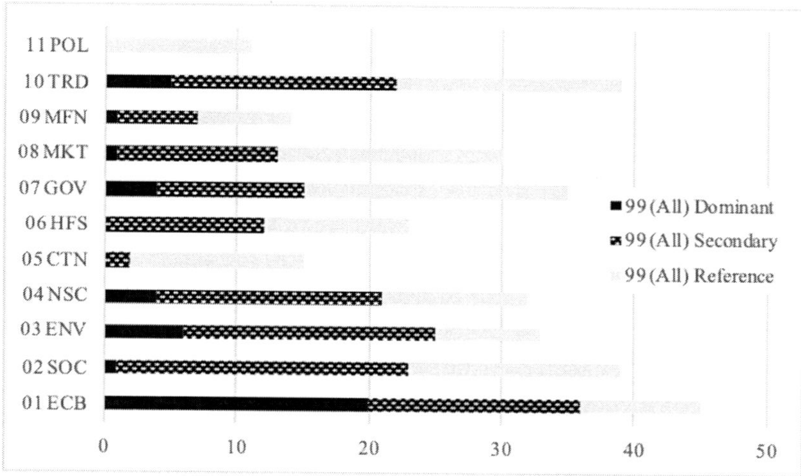

Category keyword counts

Figure 6-3 shows the frequency of keywords in each category as a percentage of the total of all keywords in each corpus of articles for both periods. For 1961, it is seen that keywords related to economic and business constituted 47% of all keywords, followed by three other relatively frequent categories: societal wellbeing (16%), political issue (15%), and government intervention (14%). Keywords from the categories of environment (3%), market (2%), culture & tradition (2%), trade (1%) and health & food safety (1%) appeared infrequently. National security/food self-sufficiency and multifunctionality received no mentions in this period.

For 1999, economic and business-related keywords were again in the plurality, accounting for 29% of all keywords mentioned. Trade issue (14%), environment (12%), societal wellbeing (12%), national security/food self-sufficiency (9%), market (9%), and government intervention (9%) were also relatively common. Health & food safety (3%), culture & tradition (3%), multifunctionality (1%) and political issue (1%) were cited least often.

FIG. 6-3: FREQUENCY OF CATEGORY KEYWORDS

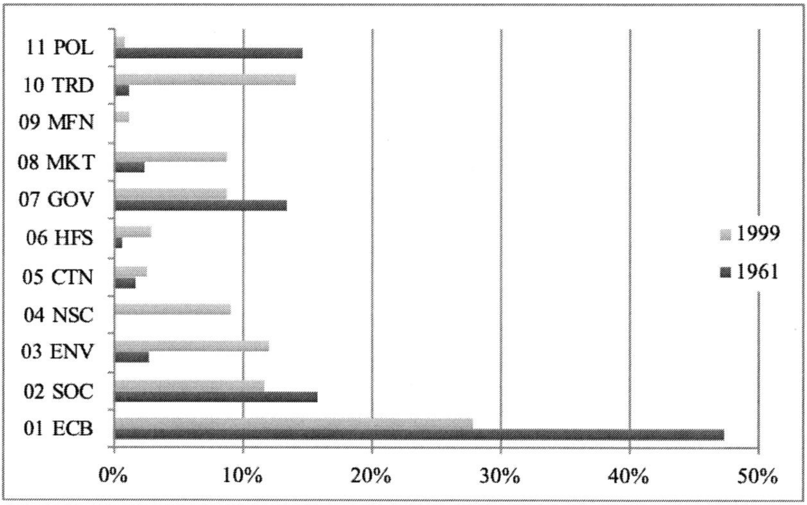

Individual keyword frequency

The results of a frequency analysis of individual keywords in each of the two corpuses of texts are presented in Table 6-2. In the 1961 corpus, in addition to agriculture (*nōgyō*), words such as rice price (*beika*), income (*shotoku*), problem (*mondai*), the Diet (*kokkai*), production (*seisan*), government (*seifu*) and rice (*kome*) are most common. In the 1999 list, in addition to agriculture, such words as country (*kuni*), production (*seisan*), Japan (*Nihon*), agricultural land (*nōchi*) and farmer (*nōka*) are most frequent.

TABLE 6-2: INDIVIDUAL KEYWORD FREQUENCY IN 1961 AND 1999

	1961		1999	
	WORD	TRANSLATION	WORD	TRANSLATION
1	農業	agriculture	農業	agriculture
2	米価	rice price	国	country
3	米	rice	生産	production
4	所得	income	新	new
5	問題	problem	日本	Japan
6	国会	the Diet	農地	agricultural land
7	生産	production	農家	farmer
8	政府	government	政策	policy
9	政策	policy	食料	foodstuff
10	審議	discussion	基本法	basic law
11	経済	economy	経営	management
12	経営	management	自給率	self-sufficiency rate
13	食管	Food Control	輸入	import
14	農民	farmer	農政	agricultural administration
15	国民	citizens	問題	problem
16	基本法	basic law	環境	environment
17	法案	draft bill	所得	income
18	制度	system	必要	necessary
19	農家	farmer	価格	price
20	価格	price	国民	citizens

6.5 Assessing the Framing of Farming

The results relating to the 1961 agricultural basic law suggest that agriculture was portrayed in relatively simple, homogenous terms in the period. Non-economic frames were marginally more common, with agriculture frequently being portrayed as an issue of governmental intervention or societal wellbeing, consistent with contemporary concerns about rapid social change. However, the economic & business and market frames also occurred with some frequency, as both dominant and secondary frames. This points towards the conclusion that, although agriculture was often framed in non-economic terms, the economic and business aspects of the modern farming sector were still widely considered by newspapers on both the left and right of the political spectrum. There is also a cross-spectrum heterodoxy of framing in evidence, in that both the Yomiuri and Asahi utilise both economic and non-economic frames with similar frequency.

The results for the 1999 period indicate that agriculture was portrayed in much more diverse ways than in the 1961 period. Overall, the economic & business frame was the most common dominant frame and also occurred frequently as a secondary frame, along with market. This implies an overall shift towards framing agriculture as a normal sector of the economy, qualitatively similar to other sectors. At the same time, non-economic frames continued to be important, with societal wellbeing, environment, and national security among the most frequent secondary frames. This suggests that even when economic concerns were being articulated as of primary importance, editorial writers typically connected their discussions to other issues, underlining the view that agriculture and agricultural policies were framed in what might appropriately be termed multifunctional ways going beyond simple economic welfare calculations.

A further notable point of the 1999 results was the continued heterodoxy of frames utilised by newspapers across the political spectrum. On the left of the spectrum, the Asahi most often framed agriculture as primarily an environmental issue, but the economic & business and market categories also appeared often as both dominant and secondary frames. For the Mainichi, economic & business and national security were the most common dominant frames, with societal wellbeing, economic & business, and environment occurring as secondary frames. For the Yomiuri, economic & business was again the main dominant frame, but health & food safety was the most commonly cited secondary frame, followed by trade. For the business-focused Nikkei, economic & business was the most frequent dominant frame, while national security and societal wellbeing were the major secondary frames, followed by environment.

The results of the category keyword counts give an alternative view of the framing of agriculture in newspaper editorials from the two periods. While a simple word-count of category keywords stripped of context does not allow the reader to differentiate between positive/supportive or negative/critical usages, the greater range of patterns and relative frequencies between the two periods still tells an important story about how agriculture was discussed. It is seen that keywords related to only four categories (economic and business, societal wellbeing, government intervention and political issue) account for over 90% of all keywords in 1961. In contrast in 1999, four categories scored over 10%, and a further three around 9%. The increased range of patterns underlines the fact that agriculture was portrayed in more diverse terms in the second period. The percentage changes evident between specific categories over the two periods also speak to how policy-related concerns changed over time, and how new ideas like multifunctionality had emerged by the 1990s.

In the individual keyword count gives further granular detail. Overall, for the 1961 period, words like rice price, income and the Diet suggest an emphasis on the societal wellbeing aspects of farming and the government's role in the sector. In the 1999 period, words such as country, agricultural land, production and Japan suggest a stressing of the business side of farming, as well as the international dimension of agriculture, contrasting Japan with other countries. Comparing the relative frequencies of specific words in the two periods also gives information about the changing degree of emphasis. Notably, production is more common in 1999, while income is much more frequent in 1961. Rice price, the Diet, deficit (*akaji*), and population (*jinkō*) are among the words to appear only in the 1961 list. In 1999, foodstuffs (*shokuryō*), self-sufficiency rate (*jikyūritsu*), imports (*yunyū*) and environment (*kankyō*) are among words appearing for the first time.

******

This chapter has examined the role of ideas about agriculture in the postwar period through a content analysis of newspaper editorial articles relating to policy debates around the two agricultural basic laws of 1961 and 1999. The primary purpose was to test the relative importance of economic versus non-economic categories in the framing of agriculture and agricultural policy in these widely-read mass-media sources, to better understand the nature and development of ideas about agriculture in the postwar era. A secondary purpose was to illustrate the role of newspapers as vectors of ideas.

The results of the framing analysis from the 1961 period show a relatively simple, homogenous portrayal of agriculture, with five categories identified. Non-economic frames were slightly more common than economic as dominant frames, but a concern about the economic and business aspects was also reflected in both dominant and secondary frames. In 1999, the results show a more diverse framing of the sector, with eleven categories identified. Economic & business was the most common dominant frame, but non-economic frames such as societal well-being, environment, and national security were common secondary frames. In both periods, a cross-spectrum heterodoxy is evident, and newspapers on both the right and left politically framed the issue in diverse ways.

The word counts of category keywords and all words in the articles in each of the two periods add further evidence to support the findings of the framing analysis. The quantitative methods employed show that words relating to societal wellbeing issues and government and politics were most common in the first period, while a greater diversity of words, many relating to economic aspects, were in evidence in the second period. Both the qualitative and quantitative methods indicate the relative categorical homogeneity of portrayals in the former period giving way to a greater diversity in the second period and the emergence of new categories.

This analysis provides solid evidence for the second stage of the theoretical framework outlined in Chapter 4. It demonstrates the kinds of ideas that were evident in public policy debates at two important turning points in modern agricultural policy history and shows the continuity and development of those ideas over time. The results support the hypothesis that agriculture has been conceived of as a complex, multi-faceted issue, with political, economic, social, and other dimensions, and that economic welfare was only one of many ideas given consideration in agricultural policy debates. The articles examined here also illustrate how newspapers may act as a vector for the transmission of ideas.

Having traced the history of ideas about agriculture from Tokugawa beginnings through the Meiji Restoration into the earlier twentieth century, and then having demonstrated their usage and development in public policy discourse in the postwar era, the final step is to consider ideas in contemporary Japan and show their relationship with the policy preferences of individuals. The next chapter examines evidence for the third and fourth stages of the theoretical framework—values and preferences towards agriculture and agricultural policy—through the analysis of public opinion survey data.

CHAPTER 7

IDEAS AMONG VOTERS: VIEWS ABOUT AGRICULTURE TODAY

How is agriculture viewed by voters in Japan today? What ideas about agriculture predominate? Are non-economic or economic ideas more influential in shaping policy preferences towards? This chapter answers these questions by analysing public opinion survey data about attitudes towards agriculture, preferences regarding agricultural policy and trade liberalisation, and the dominant ideas or images that individuals hold about agriculture.

The chapter draws upon both historical and original data from public opinion surveys related to agriculture and rural areas during the period 1975 to 2015. The former date came at a point when the cornerstone gentan policy had been in place for around five years, causing rice production to surge even as per capita annual consumption had started to decline. The latter date marked the peak of the intense public policy debates prior to the conclusion of the Trans Pacific Partnership, a major turning point in Japan's transition from a bilateral to a mega regional trade policy stance involving greater agricultural concessions.

Despite the policy re-orientation that resulted from the 1999 basic law, the agricultural sector continued to decline steadily in the 2000s and 2010s. The average age of farmers was 66.1 in the agricultural ministry's most recent 'census' of the agricultural sector.[70] The depopulation of rural areas and the shortage of successors contributed to levels of abandoned land reaching 396,000 hectares in 2010, almost double the 1990 level (Ozawa, 2017). With high production costs and low productivity relative to domestic industry, Japanese farmers remained uncompetitive in international markets and heavily reliant on governmental supports and trade protection.

In response, after taking office in December 2012, the administration of Abe Shinzō announced a series of policy goals and reforms for agriculture. The targets and measures included income doubling for the sector as a whole, doubling of the value of agricultural exports, the creation of a farmland bank and reforms to the land sales system, increased corporate involvement in farming enterprises, and reforms to JA to reduce its revenues and sectoral influence. It was also announced that the gentan policy would be phased out, although in parallel subsidies for the production of feed rice would be increased. These reform attempts are analysed in Chapter 8.

When Japan joined the TPP negotiations in March 2013, the government promised to protect the sacred *sei'iki* categories of rice, wheat and barley, beef and pork, sugar and starch crops, and dairy products (Harris, 2020, 261). However, it was clear by 2015 that this protection would not be absolute. As such, national policy debates at this time were characterised by great uncertainty about the outcomes and impacts of the TPP on agriculture and fundamental concern about the future viability of the farming sector.

7.1 Opinion Surveys and Popular Opinion

Opinion surveys offer a useful means for understanding popular views on a policy topic, given their potential to reach large numbers of individuals. As noted in the previous chapter, scholars of agenda setting use opinion surveys to study the public agenda, namely the hierarchy of concerns expressed by the general public. A drawback of traditional survey methods like in-person, telephone, or mail-in surveys was the cost, in terms of time, money, and capacity, which is why surveys were often implemented only by larger organisations. Today, the internet has helped broaden access to opinion surveys as a research tool, and online surveys offer a number of improvements over traditional methods, including the potential for larger sample sizes, greater targeting for more representative samples, timeliness, and the ability to implement path-dependent survey logics. On the other hand, online surveys do create new issues, such as the representativeness of the internet-literate demographics (particularly among older respondents).

In Japan, attitudes towards agriculture and food have been a topic for opinion surveys for many years. Typically, these surveys have found home preference to be strong. For example, in a 1988 Yomiuri poll 57% of respondents supported agricultural protection and 37% opposed it, while 59% opposed liberalisation and 32% supported it (Vogel, 1999, 193). In a 2020 survey by the Japan Finance Corporation, 66.5% of respondents thought that Japanese food was expensive and 63% thought imported food was cheap, but while 68.5% thought Japanese food was safe, only 4.4% thought imported food was safe.[71]

This negative view of imports derives in part from a series of imported food scandals that occurred in Japan in recent years. These include imported Chinese spinach containing high levels of pesticides in 2002, [72] the deliberate poisoning of imported gyoza dumplings in 2008 that sickened dozens of consumers, food poisoning related to pickled Chinese cabbage in 2012, and problems with imported chicken meat from Shanghai and fish products from Vietnam in 2014 (Kasai, 2015). However, domestically produced food was not without its own problems in these years. Notable incidents included more than 14,000 people being sickened by milk produced by Snow Brand Foods in 2000, the mislabelling of meat products at the Meat Hope company in Hokkaido in 2007, and the deaths of four people after consuming raw meat in branches of a chain restaurant in early 2011. Perhaps most infamously, the March 2011 nuclear power plant disaster at Fukushima caused contamination of agricultural land in that region.

7.2 Cabinet Office Surveys about Agriculture and Food

One of the most useful sources of longitudinal data for Japanese consumer attitudes towards food and agriculture comes from the series of public opinion surveys conducted on a range of policy areas by the Cabinet Office (*Naikakufu*). Since 1975, twelve of these surveys have related directly to the nexus of agriculture and food.[73] While specific wordings or questions varied over time, many themes remained constant in multiple surveys, allowing for useful longitudinal comparison. Summarised extracts from these twelve surveys are presented in Table 7.1, while further details are given in Appendix II.[74]

Domestic food versus imports

First, many questions dealt with issues relating to domestically produced food vis-à-vis imported food. Throughout the period, a clear majority of respondents were concerned with low food self-sufficiency and high levels of imports (Row 1), while even higher numbers were concerned about future food supply when asked in 2000 and after. On the question of imported food versus domestic production (Row 2), home preference strongly outweighed price considerations. Support for imports when cheaper started at a low level and declined even further throughout the period, while support for domestic production of all food or just basic food items even if more expensive each consistently averaged around 40% support. Looking at the reasons for home preference (Row 3), when asked, on average over 80% cited safety, over 60% cited freshness, and over 50% cited quality. In terms of overall image in relation to these three considerations (Row 4), Japanese agricultural products were seen on average as expensive but safe and fresh by almost 50%, not so expensive and safe and fresh by a little under 20%, and expensive but not especially safe or fresh by around 10%.

Roles of agriculture and rural areas

Second, a range of questions dealt with the roles of agriculture and rural areas. On the roles of rural areas (Row 5), when asked, on average around 70% of respondents said food production, around 30% environmental protection, and close to 20% maintaining culture, festivals, and tradition. Among urban residents in the 1987 survey, over 70% considered protection of the environment and nature to be the role of rural areas. In the 1990 survey, over 50% of respondents mentioned reducing pesticides and providing stable food as a role of rural areas and agriculture, while only 20% cited the need to address consumer needs. Finally, on the main role of agriculture, on average just under 30% of the respondents thought that economic efficiency was most important since agriculture is one part of the economy, while over 40% thought that functions like land and environmental protection were more important though economic efficiency should also be improved, and a little over 10% said that land and environmental protection functions outweighed economic efficiency.

TABLE 7-1: EXTRACTS FROM CABINET OFFICE SURVEYS, 1975-2014

Row	Item		1975	1978	1980	1984	1987	1990	1993	1996	2000	2007	2009	2014
1	Concern with:	low FSS / high imports	66.7			56.7		62.8	71.0	70.5		70.1	79.1	
		future food supply									78.4	76.7	93.5	
2	Imports vs. domestic production:	imports when cheaper		20.1	16.4	14.1	19.9	17.0	17.4	10.8	10.5	7.8	3.1	
		domestic food, while reducing production price, even if price is higher					31.9	32.7	32.4	45.9	43.6	44.5	51.5	
		domestic basics like rice, while reducing production price, even if price is higher					39.6	40.5	44.7	37.5	40.6	42.3	42.4	
3	Reason for home preference:	freshness						70.6	69.4	66.6	57.3		51.6	
		quality								57.8	42.3		56.7	
		safety								71.7	82.0		89.1	
4	Domestic agriculture is relatively:	expensive but provides fresh, safe food						51.1	44.3	53.6				
		expensive but doesn't provide fresh, safe food						13.0	10.7	8.4				
		not so expensive and provides fresh, safe food						12.5	22.4	19.0				
5	Role of rural areas:	food production						63.4	73.2	74.9			65.8	83.4
		providing livelihoods						30.0	36.0	29.7			46.1	48.7
		environmental protection or nature				56.6	*70.9			23.6			48.9	49.8
		reduce pesticides, provide stable food						54.2						

		address consumer needs			22.4						
		maintain culture, festivals, tradition	23.8	*11.4			12.6				
		provide fresh food	50.8	*32.1							
6	On agricultural areas, economic role and future:	economic efficiency is most important as agriculture is one part of economy				30.6	26.8			9.3	13.7
		functions like land and environmental protection most important, while improving economic efficiency				42.4	42.2			68.2	63.1

Source: Cabinet Offices website (see Appendix II for details).
Notes: All figures are percentages. All questions were multiple choice with fixed response. Some questions permitted multiple selections, so the sum of responses may exceed 100. Some responses reported in the same time series are collated from similar but differently-worded questions from different years. Numbers marked with an asterisk (*) indicate responses from urban residents only (1987); in all other surveys, answers from both urban and rural residents were reported together.

In sum, the Cabinet Office survey data set reveals important trends in how the public has viewed agriculture and food in recent decades. First, price appears to have been a relatively low concern for respondents comparing domestic and imported produce. Second, supply-related concerns have been strong, in terms of both current food self-sufficiency and future supply. Third, regarding reasons for preferring domestic produce, risk-related factors like quality and safety scored highly, along with freshness. Fourth, rural areas have been valued highly for their food production function, with environmental protection and their cultural role also cited. More respondents thought that land and environmental protection was equally or more important for agriculture than its economic role. Taken together, these data support the view that non-material factors have trumped material factors like price in shaping consumer preferences towards agriculture and food.

7.3 An Original Survey of Ideas about Agriculture

To investigate more deeply the values and preferences of contemporary voters towards agriculture and related policy issues, this section presents the results of an original public opinion survey conducted online in Japan prior to the conclusion of the TPP agreement in 2015. The survey was conducted under the auspices of the Asia Pacific Institute of Research in Osaka, and is published here with kind permission.[75] The sample size of 500 was designed to be representative of in terms of gender, age, and prefecture of residence. Topics included scenarios related to loss in the context of trade liberalisation, and questions on ideas, images, and keywords associated with agriculture. The results are presented in three parts: (1) comparing potential loss scenarios for agricultural and other items, (2) protecting agriculture in trade negotiations, and (3) overall images of agriculture and related keywords.

Relative strength of sentiment towards agriculture

The first question asked respondents how they would feel in response to each of ten scenarios of loss, concerning the domestic production of five agricultural and three manufacturing goods, plus two culturally meaningful aspects of society—*satoyama-no-fūkei* (traditional village scenery, typically involving rice paddies and hills), and the emperor system, perhaps Japan's most important cultural institution, itself with deep historical roots and connections to agriculture (as noted in Chapter 5).[76] While loss aversion is to be expected as a common psychological phenomenon, the purpose of these questions was to reveal the relative strength of sentiment for agriculture-related items compared to other items with high levels of economic or cultural importance.

As shown in Figure 7-1, the number of respondents who reported that they would be very or somewhat disappointed at the potential loss were 85% for rice production, 83% for pharmaceuticals production, 82% for satoyama-no-fūkei, 81% for beef or pork production, 80% for dairy production, 78% for paper production, 75% for wheat production, 71% for sugar production, 65% for semiconductor production, and 52% for the emperor system.

As expected, loss aversion was strong for all items. Rice production received the highest number of responses for very disappointing (77%) as well as for the combined very or somewhat disappointing. Satoyama-no-fūkei also scored very highly in both very disappointing (69%) and very or somewhat disappointing. Both these results provide evidence for the special position of agriculture and especially rice in public opinion, and suggest that the image of rice paddies as forming a quintessential part of the Japanese countryside is almost as esteemed as the commodity itself. Looking at other agricultural products, it is seen that the other sei'iki categories in TPP negotiations all provoked strong sentiment among respondents, ranging from 71% to 81%. Paper, a manufactured product of the forestry sector, was also highly ranked.

This sentiment favouring agricultural products is particularly striking when contrasted with the response for semi-conductors (65% either very or somewhat disappointed), the second-lowest figure of all ten items despite being a much more valuable product in economic terms. Indeed, the only item for which scoring broadly matched economic importance was pharmaceuticals, which gained responses of 69% very and 14% somewhat disappointing. It may be the case that this response reflects a perceived national security importance to a country producing its own medicines, as much as a recognition of its economic significance, although further data would be required to test this hypothesis.

Finally, the relatively low response to the possible loss of the emperor system, which had been included because of its cultural importance and historical linkages to agriculture, was unexpected. Despite the significance of the emperor system with a purported lineage stretching over two millennia and a position underscored by the postwar constitution, this result seems to suggest that the contemporary voters exhibit stronger sentiment towards rice.

FIG. 7-1: VIEWS ON POTENTIAL LOSS SCENARIOS

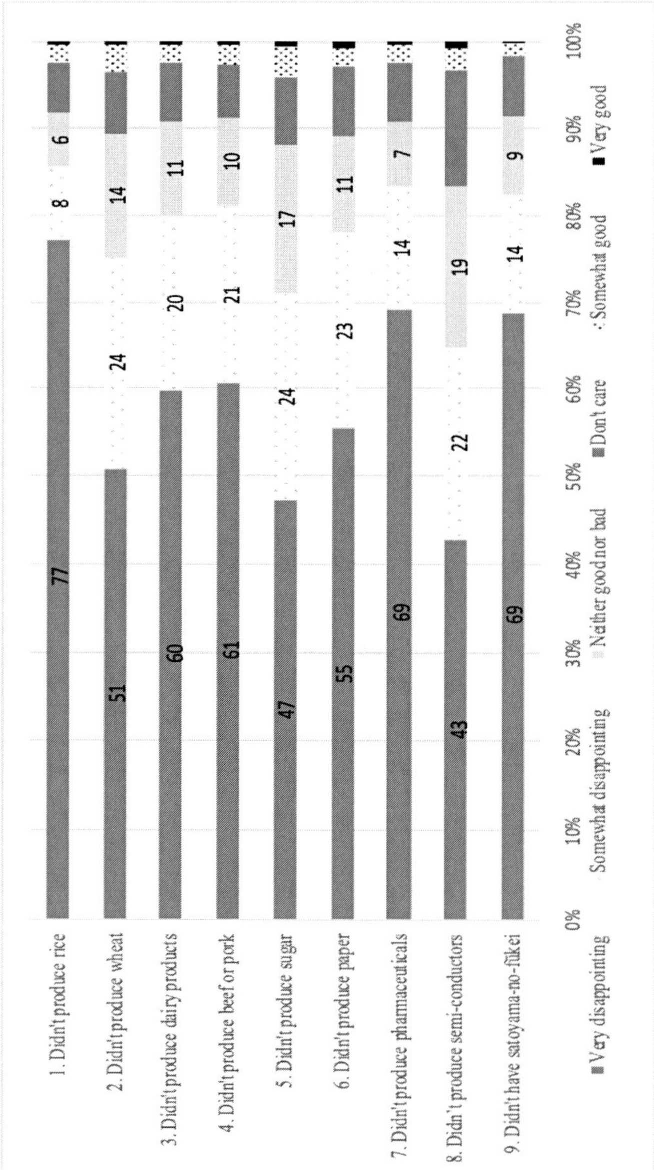

Protecting agriculture in trade negotiations

The next set of questions concerned trade negotiations and protectionism, and included path-dependent logics. When asked generally whether the Japanese government should protect any sectors in trade negotiations, 74% of respondents answered yes, and 26% no. A subsequent question asked which sectors should be protected; for ease of comparison, the numbers for and against protecting each sector are reported as percentages of the total sample, with those against the protection of any sectors included in the opposing responses for each category.

As shown in Figure 7-2, the sectors that a majority wished to see protected in trade negotiations were agriculture, forestry, and fisheries (66%), medical services (55%), and government procurement (52%). Electronics manufacturing (43%), chemical industries (39%), and retail and trade (39%) were in the middle range, while finance and insurance (36%), construction (36%), other manufacturing (36%), and automobile manufacturing (36%) gained lower responses.

Again, these responses indicate that agriculture enjoys by far the highest levels of public sentiment in favour of protection in trade negotiations, with two-thirds of all respondents favouring special treatment, more than ten percentage points ahead of the second-highest ranking sector, medical services. Of the respondents who favoured protecting some sector in trade negotiations, 90% favoured protection for agriculture.

The next set of questions sought to uncover the reasons why respondents wanted either to see agriculture protected or to see it liberalised—which links strongly to the ideas or values shaping protectionist sentiment towards agriculture. First, the survey asked directly: "Do you agree or disagree that the agricultural sector should be excluded from liberalisation when Japan participates in trade agreements?" To this, 56% responded agree, and 44% disagree. Based on these answers, respondents were then asked to give the single reason that most closely expressed their views for or against excluding agriculture from liberalisation. Figures 7-3 and 7-4 show the responses to each sub-question, once again given as percentages of the entire sample.

FIG. 7-2: SECTORS DESERVING PROTECTION IN TRADE NEGOTIATIONS

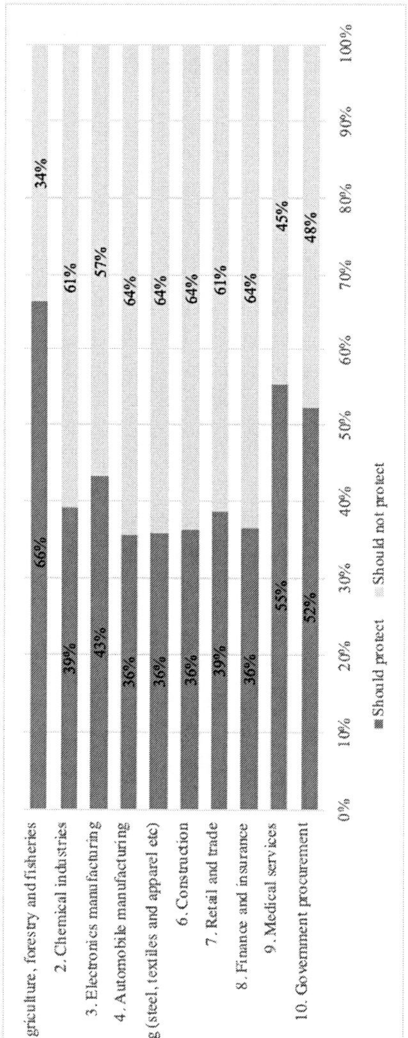

FIG. 7-3: REASONS FOR EXCLUDING AGRICULTURE FROM LIBERALISATION

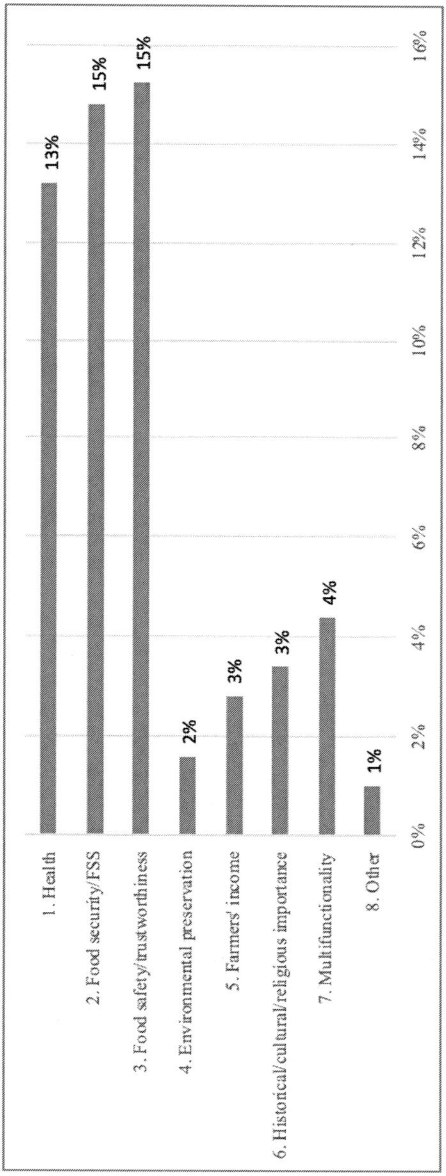

As seen in Figure 7-3, the most commonly selected reason for wishing to exclude agriculture was “Because Japanese food is safer and/or more trustworthy than imports,” chosen by 15% of all respondents, closely followed by “The government has a responsibility to ensure that people have a secure source of food and that they have access to food grown domestically.” “Because food is important for maintaining health” was selected by 13%. Among other answers, 4% gave the multifunctionality (beyond food production) of agriculture, 3% cited the historical, cultural and/or religious importance of agriculture in society, 3% said that farmers should have a steady income even if it requires government help, 2% cited the role of farmers in protecting the environment, and 1% selected “other”.

These figures indicate that three concerns clearly dominate among those who favour protecting agriculture: food safety, national security (in terms of food self-sufficiency), and health. Together, health and food safety account for the primary concerns of 28% of all respondents. These numbers are consistent with other survey data regarding the importance of food safety. The second-most common response, concerning the government’s role to ensure a secure supply of food, recalls the governmentality argument advanced by Barclay and Epstein (2013) and discussed in Chapter 1, that securing food for the nation is popularly understood as a central area of responsibility of the modern state. The relative lack of concern with farmers’ incomes (only 3%) contrasts with the findings of Naoi and Kume (2011) regarding individuals projecting their own job insecurity onto farmers as a significant reason for supporting agricultural protection. Among the less common reasons cited, the response for multifunctionality is of interest since it is a relatively new concept, dating only from the mid-1990s.

Among respondents who wished to see agriculture liberalised, shown in Figure 7-4, the three top reasons were because of the high cost of food (8.8% of the total sample), that agricultural protectionism was excessive (also 8.8%), and in order to increase consumer choice of food products (8.2%). Less common reasons included extending the market principle (5%), because protectionism benefits politically influential groups (3.8%), and in order to participate in FTAs, boost trade, and help Japan’s internationally competitive industries (3.4%).

FIG. 7-4: REASONS FOR INCLUDING AGRICULTURE IN LIBERALISATION

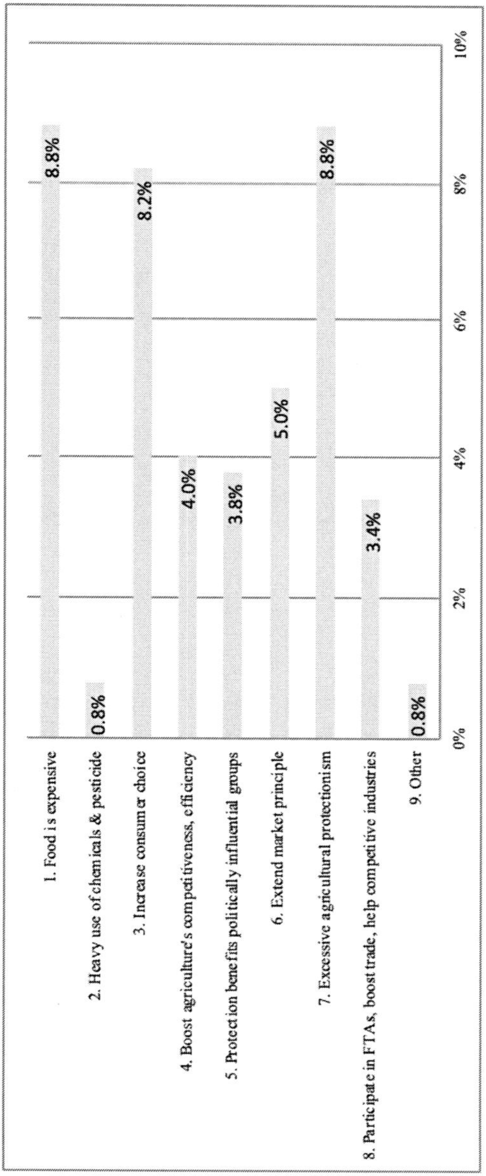

Images of agriculture

The next questions asked respondents about the images they hold about agriculture—first, to rate each of ten categories, then to select the idea most strongly associated with the image they hold. The categories of ideas were based on the categories used in the newspaper editorial analysis undertaken in Chapter 6, and the questions were designed to parallel the 'secondary' and 'dominant' frames analysed in that chapter.

Figure 7-5 shows the responses for each of the ten categories. The number of respondents who thought that health and food safety was *strongly* or *somewhat* related to their image of agriculture was 74%, the highest-scoring response. Other answers chosen by a majority of respondents were Japanese culture and tradition (68%), national security (e.g. food self-sufficiency) (65%), and environmental protection (59%). Trade protection is needed was selected by 49%, followed by trade problem and multifunctional industry (each 48%), and a normal industrial sector (45%). The lowest-ranked of all ten categories was trade liberalisation is needed, with 33%, while conversely this category received the highest score for not very or not at all related, with 50%.

FIG. 7-5: IMAGES ASSOCIATED WITH AGRICULTURE

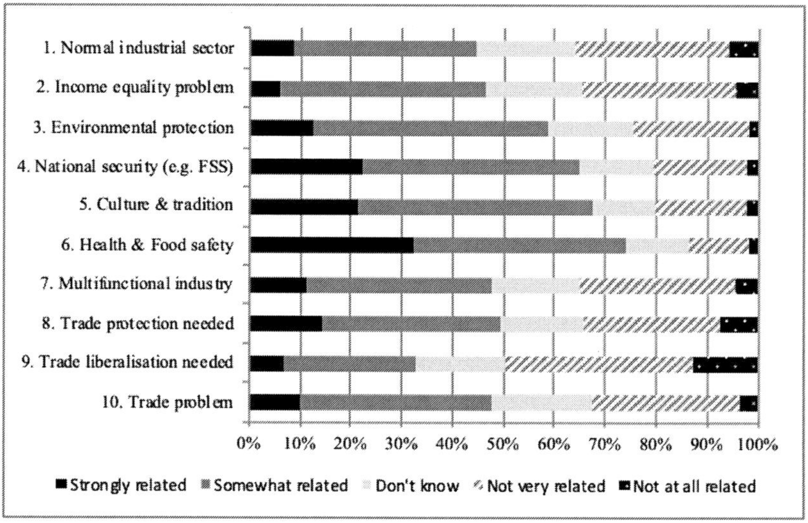

The most strongly associated images are shown in Figure 7-6.[77] The three most commonly selected responses were health & food safety, chosen by 28% of the total sample, followed by national security (e.g. food self-sufficiency) (18%), and Japanese culture and tradition' (12%). Among the less commonly selected categories, trade liberalisation is needed was chosen by 6%, multifunctional industry by 4%, income equality problem by 4%, and a normal industrial sector by 3%. Finally, trade protection is needed was selected by 2% of the total sample, environmental protection by 2%, and trade problem by 1%.

Taken together, these two sets of results give more detailed information about the underlying ideas and values that shape attitudes towards agriculture and agricultural policy. The health & food safety category received the plurality of responses for both questions, with almost three-quarters of respondents seeing it as strongly or somewhat related, and 28% viewing it as the single most relevant issue. This figure mirrors the combined 28% who cited either health or food safety as the reason why agriculture should be excluded from liberalisation, seen in Figure 7-3. The high levels of responses for Japanese culture and tradition in both questions was somewhat unanticipated, but is perhaps less surprising in light of the strong sentiment previously expressed towards satoyama-no-fūkei in Figure 7-1. National security was also a major concern among respondents, perhaps reflecting the inherent appeal of the idea of food self-sufficiency in an island nation. Combined with the very low responses for a normal industrial sector, these findings are further evidence in support of the hypothesis that agriculture is considered an exceptional sector of the economy with special cultural and historical importance.

Responses to the less-frequently selected categories also offer useful insights. For example, 7% of respondents thought that trade liberalisation is needed was strongly related to agriculture, and 6% cited trade liberalisation as their strongest single image, suggesting that for most of those who support agricultural trade liberalisation it is their major concern. Taken together, the three trade-related categories were among the lowest-scoring of all ten in both questions. Thus, while Japanese agriculture is predominantly viewed as a trade issue in international trade negotiations and international media discourse, agricultural trade appears to be a low concern for Japanese voters, who view their nation's agricultural sector in terms of its connection to their own lives and culture. In addition, environmental protection ranked fourth-highest for the first question, but second-lowest for the second question, indicating that it is a general concern for many respondents in relation to agriculture, but the primary concern for very few people.

To compare media portrayals and public opinion, Figure 7-7 offers a comparison between the dominant themes identified in Chapter 6's analysis of newspaper editorials in the 1999 period and the most strongly associated images cited by respondents to this online survey, each expressed as a percentage of the sum of all occurrences within each grouping. The categories from each data set are aligned with the most closely corresponding category from the other.

Clear discrepancies are observed in almost every category. It is seen that whereas the newspaper editorials adopted business as the dominant frame in almost half of all articles, in contrast only 3% of survey respondents see agriculture mainly as a normal sector of the economy. Environment, trade issue/trade problem, and government intervention/trade protection needed show discrepancies in the same direction. Conversely, health & food safety was the primary concern for a plurality of survey respondents, and yet did not feature as the dominant frame in a single editorial. Discrepancies are also visible for culture & tradition, societal wellbeing/income equality, and market/trade liberalisation.

The only categories for which frequency for the two sets of data somewhat matched were for national security/food self-sufficiency (10% in editorials, 18% in the survey) and multifunctionality (4% in editorials, 4% in the survey). Since the data were derived from different periods and not all of the categories aligned precisely, firm conclusions cannot readily be drawn. Even so, the preponderance of discrepancies points to a divergence between media portrayals and public opinion, with voters much more focused on non-economic concerns.

The last question on the survey gave respondents the chance to freely enter words or sentences in answer to the question, "What image do you have of 'Japanese agriculture'?" Among the responses, non-material and risk-related concepts feature prominently, including "safety," "peace of mind," "quality," "self-sufficiency," "shortage," and "trust". Many respondents wrote some variation of "safe," "safe and delicious," or "absolutely safe." Some praised the quality as "high," "world-class," or "the envy of the world," while others responded that it was "reliable," "highly reliable," or "more reliable than other countries." Agrarian fundamentalist sentiment was evident in such comments as "Japan's foundation," "agriculture is the basis of everything," and "Japanese agriculture works in harmony with Japan's unique environment and reflects the nature of Japanese people."

The idea of nationality security was clear in such responses as "on the off chance a war breaks out and food stops coming into Japan, we will be in trouble if there are no people, places or industries in our country that can produce foods," and "if we cannot supply our own food, our country will collapse". The most frequently occurring words from this textual corpus are reported in Table 7-2.

FIG. 7-6: MOST STRONGLY ASSOCIATED IMAGES ABOUT AGRICULTURE

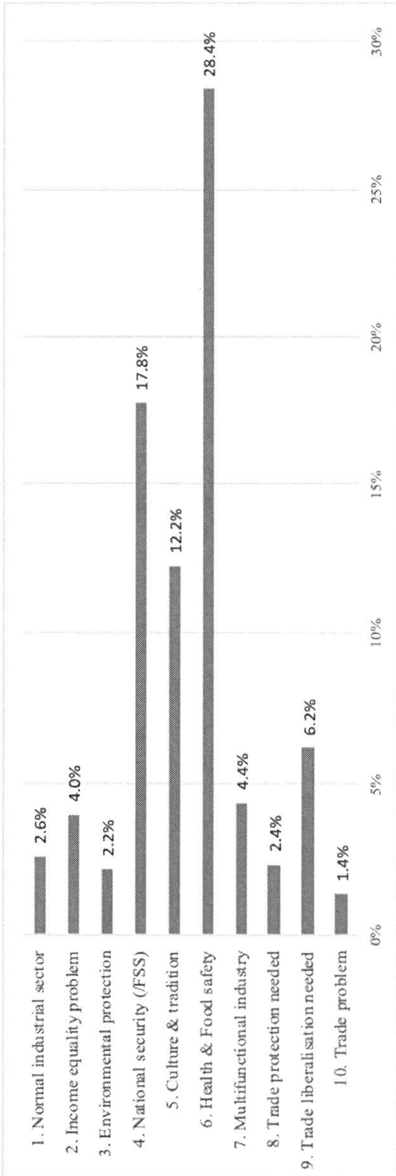

FIG. 7-7: COMPARING MEDIA FRAMES AND POPULAR IMAGES

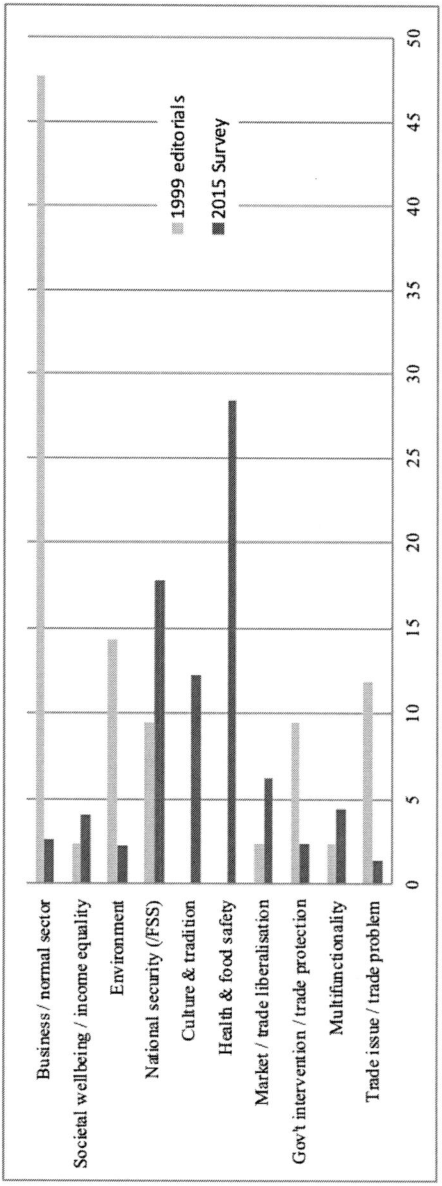

TABLE 7-2: FREE RESPONSE QUESTION ON IMAGE OF JAPANESE AGRICULTURE

Rank	Word	Translation	Freq.	Rank	Word	Translation
1	安全	safety	336	16	伝統	tradition
2	高	high, expensive	259	17	小規模	small-scale (farming)
3	食	food	241	18	高齢化	ageing (of population)
4	安心	peace of mind, safety	227	19	後継者	successors
5	保護	protection	212	20	世界	world
6	農家	farmer	187	21	不足	shortage
7	国	country, state	177	22	自由	free, freedom
8	人	person, people	158	23	食料	foodstuffs

9	米	rice	150	24	信頼	trust
10	必要	necessary	136	25	効率	efficiency
11	品質	quality	130	26	海外	overseas
12	生産	production	124	27	競争力	competitiveness
13	産業	industry	119	28	経営	management
14	農協	JA	114	29	大変	grave, serious
15	自給	self-sufficiency	109	30	土地	land

******

The data from the public opinion surveys analysed in this chapter offer valuable insights into the ideas and values that voters hold regarding agriculture in Japan. Across several decades, the twelve Cabinet Office surveys consistently demonstrate a low sensitivity to price, high concerns about food self-sufficiency and food supply, a preference for domestic food due to factors such as quality and safety, and concern about rural areas in terms of their roles in food production, environmental protection, and culture.

Those findings are reinforced by the results of the original online survey, from which three points stand out. First, in terms of sentiment, agricultural products and rural scenery are held in notably higher esteem than other sectors or products of greater economic importance, and provoke stronger sentiment than even a culturally significant institution like the emperor system. Second, in terms of images held about agriculture, the most common relate to health and food safety, culture & tradition, national security (including food self-sufficiency), and environmental protection. Third, in terms of significant ideas, ideas with primarily non-economic significance, rather than those with primarily economic importance, seem to be foremost in the minds of voters when forming their attitudes towards agriculture and agricultural policies.

Overall, these findings concerning voters in contemporary Japan are consistent with a growing body of economic literature on the importance of non-economic factors in shaping policy preferences. The results also provide important information that helps elaborate the third and fourth stages of the theoretical framework outlined in Chapter 4, demonstrating the multiple values held in relation to agriculture, which in turn shape individuals' policy preferences in favour of agricultural protection. The final chapter of this book looks at developments in agriculture during the (second) premiership of Abe Shinzō and the implications of two unfolding crises for the sector, in the context of the most important ideas identified from this public opinion survey data.

CHAPTER 8

THINKING AHEAD: JAPANESE AGRICULTURE IN THE 2020S AND BEYOND

The purpose of this book has been to establish the extent to which ideas are an important explanatory variable shaping individual policy preferences in the political economy of agriculture in Japan, through an examination of the origins, development, and modern expression of such ideas. The study has sought to demonstrated that the inclusion of ideational factors provides for a more complete account of the political economy of Japanese agriculture than accounts that focus only on material, institutional or political (self-) interests.

To this end, it reviewed the origins and development of agrarian ideas from the Tokugawa period until the first half of the twentieth century. Thinkers associated with the nōhonshugi tradition often located agriculture at the root of Japanese society, and variously articulated a range of romantic, rational, or market-oriented conceptions of the sector. A content analysis of postwar newspaper editorial portrayals of agriculture in policy debates about the 1961 and 1999 agricultural basic laws showed how ideas about agriculture continued to evolve and diversify during the second half of the twentieth century, during a period of changing circumstances domestically and internationally. This analysis found that while economic framings of agriculture became more important in the latter period, a diverse range of non-economic ideas continued to be articulated by newspapers across the political spectrum.

Finally, a study of public opinion survey data since the 1970s found evidence that popular ideas about agriculture have continued to be diverse, and that non-economic concerns predominate for a consistent majority of consumers and voters. In particular, ideas about health and food safety, food self-sufficiency, and the environment prevail over economic concerns. Across a span of four centuries and through three different methodologies, then, we find substantial evidence for the historical and contemporary prevalence and influence of the ideas outlined in the introductory chapter, relating to agriculture's role in the economy and business, history and culture, societal welfare, national security, health and food safety, and the environment, as well as certain other ideas.

As such, this study reaches three main conclusions. First, non-economic ideas about agriculture have long been important in political thought and policy debates in early-modern and modern Japan, and such ideas have often predominated over ideas emphasising agriculture's economic role. Second, non-economic ideas are an important factor that shape popular policy preferences and that must be accounted for in any comprehensive account of the political economy of agriculture in Japan. And third, in contemporary Japan, ideas relating to health and food safety, culture and tradition, food self-sufficiency, and the environment are significantly more important to voters than ideas about the economic role of agriculture.

Today, Japan's agricultural sector is in a state of crisis, with an elderly and rapidly ageing workforce, a weakening production base due to cultivation abandonment, and a shortage of successors to inherit family farms. At the same time, Japanese agriculture has faced transformative challenges at several points in modern times, notably following the Meiji Restoration and in the early postwar years, so the problems that confront the sector today are not without precedent. This concluding chapter considers the implications of the most important contemporary ideas identified in this study in the context of recent developments at the domestic and international levels and in relation to two major external challenges going forward. Section 8.1 analyses reform attempts under the recent Abe administration, while Section 8.2 considers the possible impacts of the coronavirus pandemic and anthropogenic climate change, in terms of concerns about agriculture, food, and health in Japan. Section 8.3 concludes with brief remarks on the implications of this study for scholars, policy practitioners, and others with a professional interest in the agriculture and political economy of Japan.

8.1 Prestidigitation and Reform under the Abe Administration

Deep-rooted ideas about agriculture in Japan must co-exist with the reality of domestic and global political economies in the early decades of the twenty-first century, which continue to trend towards greater liberalisation and internationalisation. Domestically, the administration of Abe Shinzō, in office from December 2012 until September 2020, articulated an expansive series of reforms for the farming sector, rural areas, and organised agricultural interests. In international relations, Japan's trade policy orientation shifted from bilateral deals in the 2000s to mega regional agreements in the 2010s, a change that impacted the domestic agricultural policy regime and reanimated debates about the long-term sustainability of the sector.

Domestic reform proposals under Abe

For the agricultural sector, the second premiership of Abe Shinzō[78] had the potential to be one of the most consequential of the modern era, given Abe's longevity in becoming Japan's longest-serving prime minister, his relative success in centralising power to create what Mulgan (2018) termed a "prime ministerial executive," and his appetite for neoliberal-type economic reforms that emphasised deregulation, marketisation, and (in permitted areas) devolved decision-making. According to his biographer Tobias Harris, for Abe, "there was no greater political challenge than agricultural reform" (Harris, 2020, 297). That challenge covered two areas—market-oriented reforms to the farming sector itself, and reforms to JA.

The market-oriented agricultural reform proposals articulated in the first years of the Abe administration were among the most ambitious since the 1950s and 1960s, and if implemented they implied a fundamental restructuring of the sector. The overarching theme was *seme no nōrinsuisangyō*[79] ('agriculture on the offensive'), an approach with roots in a mid-2000s MAFF strategy advocated by then-prime minister Koizumi Junichiro (Sasada, 2008). Under Abe, the proposals included (i) phasing out the gentan set-aside policy for rice, (ii) liberalising the land sales process, (iii) promoting corporate involvement in agriculture, including allowing land purchases, (iv) increasing agricultural sector income through doubling agricultural and food exports, and (v) the promotion of 'sixth sector industrialisation' (*dairokuji sangyōka*), the concept that primary sector producers could profit more by also engaging in secondary and tertiary activities like food processing and operating restaurants.[80]

Among broader plans to establish a series of special economic zones to promote innovation across the economy, two agricultural districts were included, with different purposes. One zone was in the demographically-declining rural municipality of Yabu in northern Hyogo prefecture, where regulations were relaxed and private corporations were encouraged to obtain land and establish new ventures such as indoor vertical farming, with a view to revitalising the local economy and society.[81] The other zone, in Niigata prefecture, would focus on innovations in large-scale rice production.

Despite the political rhetoric, the reality of these market-oriented reforms at times resembled prestidigitation more than policy-making. This was exemplified by Abe's claim that he would abolish the gentan. As noted in Chapter 2, while the set-aside program for staple rice was scaled up, subsidies for rice produced for animal feed were simultaneously increased, seemingly to reduce dependence on imported animal feed (and hence raise the food self-sufficiency level). Despite no change in overall rice planting, no decrease in the price of staple rice, and an actual increase in the overall cost of the subsidy programmes for the taxpayer, Abe still received credit in the media for 'ending' the gentan.[82]

Similarly, the export-doubling plan overlooked the very different structure of Japan's agricultural and food exports compared to the structure of domestic agricultural production, the former being dominated by processed items such as alcoholic beverages and high value/low volume exports like prime meats and shellfish. Primary domestic farm products overall amounted to less than one-quarter of total agricultural and food exports by value in 2014, while the shares for individual farm products were 2.7% (24.7 billion yen) for beef, 1.7% (15.3 billion yen) for green tea, 1.5% (14 billion yen) for apples, and only 0.4% (3.8 billion yen) for rice in 2018.[83] Although steady progress was made towards the government's export target throughout the Abe years, doubling the value of such items would in practice have little effect on the majority of farmers, who continued to focus heavily on rice production.

If the market-oriented reforms were superficial, the proposed reforms to JA represented "a far more substantive battle" (Solis, 2017, 155). These proposals were part of what Abe portrayed as his strategy of drilling through the "solid bedrock" of regulations and vested interests inhibiting growth in the national economy, with the prime minister himself claiming the role of the drill bit.[84] Shifting power from the centralised JA structures was intended to allow regional cooperatives to play a greater role in innovation, and boost the international competitiveness of the farming industry (Mulgan, 2016).

Through a report by its Regulatory Reform Council in May 2014, the administration initially proposed extensive reforms to JA, including ending

JA's exemption from the anti-monopoly law, removing the right of its peak political organisation JA-Zenchū to collect levies from local cooperatives, and limiting associate membership for non-farmers (Solis, 2017, 155). These associate members provide the basis for the profitable activities of JA's financial arms, which cross-subsidise the loss-making farm-related operations (Mulgan, 2016). Other peak bodies would also face reforms, such as JA-Zennoh becoming a joint-stock company.

Following talks with agricultural policy tribe politicians, the administration compromised on most points. JA-Zenchū would lose its exemptions and become a general incorporated association no longer able to collect levies from below, but prefectural cooperatives would retain their status and levy-collecting abilities and hence could fund JA-Zenchū indirectly.[85] Local cooperatives would be able to choose between being audited by JA-Zenchū or independent firms, the decision on the privatisation of JA-Zennoh would be left to the organisation itself, and on the question of associate members, the decision would be deferred. As with the market-oriented policies, Abe could claim to have made reforms to JA in line with his proposals, without having effected much meaningful change to a still-powerful political interest group.

Trade policy reforms

Starting under the DPJ and continuing under Abe, Japan's trade policy orientation gradually shifted from bilateral deals in the 2000s to a series of mega agreements in the 2010s that each encompassed at least 40% of global GDP, including the TPP-12 agreement and subsequent 11-member CPTPP, the Japan-EU EPA, the U.S.-Japan FTA, and the 15-member RCEP agreement. These agreements represented a departure for a country that had previously eschewed negotiations with major economies and leading agricultural exporters. Mireya Solis termed it a "remarkable transformation of Japanese trade policy… from dedicated multilateralist and passive rule-taker to become an active preferential trader and proponent of new disciplines on trade and investment" (Solis, 2017, 128).

These mega agreements involved a greater degree of agricultural liberalisation, implemented incrementally, as detailed in Chapter 2. For example, under the CPTPP tariffs were reduced on items including beef, pork, dairy products, and sugar, and tariff-free quotas were increased for rice and durum wheat (see Table 2-1). In the case of beef, tariffs would be reduced from 38% to 9% over a period of fifteen years. Japanese producers of these items could see increasing levels of competition in that period, which could drive some productivity gains. However, any potential gains would likely be mitigated by the generous countermeasures promised by the administration, starting with 3 trillion yen for beef producers. In scale and nature, they recalled the 6 trillion yen of expenditure that followed the 1994 Uruguay Round agreement, which failed to bring about lasting structural or productivity improvements in the sector.

Overall, agricultural policy and agricultural trade policy under the Abe administration did little to improve the agricultural sector in relation to consumer and voter preferences relating to health and food safety, food self-sufficiency, and the environment. Domestically, the producer-focused reform plans articulated the goal of boosting farmer incomes to improve the economic viability of the sector, but the preferred policy instruments remained inefficient and often self-defeating. Political reforms also failed to make substantive changes to the role of JA. Internationally, tariff reductions could lead to increased competition and drive productivity gains in a few sectors, but the generous countermeasures should mitigate the effects of foreign competition, while the bulk of the farming sector, still focused on rice production, will continue to see little impact.

8.2 Two Crises for Japan's Food Security

From Meiji-era proponents through postwar policy debates to contemporary voters and consumers, the idea of securing the domestic food supply has long had a strong resonance in Japan. The idea is generally articulated as *food self-sufficiency*, the share of Japan's total food needs that are produced domestically. Food self-sufficiency is calculated and reported on a calorie basis, implying a national security purpose, rather than on a monetary value basis, which would be an economic statistic. Related concepts include *food security*, which in Japan is taken to mean the physical ability to access daily nutrition (implying a preference for domestic produce as more easily physically accessible), whereas the Food and Agriculture Organisation of the United Nations (FAO) uses the term to mean having the resources to access sufficient food each day, regardless of whether that food is sourced domestically or internationally.[86] Similarly, the concept of *food sovereignty* encompasses government policies to achieve food self-sufficiency or domestic food security. At root, concerns about food self-sufficiency and food security in Japan are concerns about how to feed the nation during a major crisis.

Agriculture and food during a pandemic

The rapid spread of the novel coronavirus COVID-19 in 2020 precipitated the worst global public health crisis in over a century. According to the World Health Organisation, identified cases rose from 100 all in China in January to over 30 million confirmed infections and around 1 million deaths across more than 200 countries or territories by September of that year.[87] More than half of global cases in the period occurred in just three countries—the United States (7 million), India (5.5 million) and Brazil (4.5 million). In comparison, the statistics for Japan were well below those for other high-income or highly-populous nations—around 80,000 cases and 1,500 deaths in the same period. In addition to the human costs, patterns of daily life were disrupted globally, and the virus had a significant impact on national economies and the networks of production, processing, and services that underpin them. As the first wave of the virus peaked, second-quarter output declined by 20.4% in the United Kingdom, 11.7% in the EU-27 area, 9.1% in the United States, and by 7.8% in Japan.[88]

Around the world, agriculture sectors and food supply systems were significantly affected. The pandemic placed unprecedented stress on food supply chains, according to the OECD.[89] Stephens et al. noted that the impacts would include (1) food security due to the impact on food distribution channels and stay-at-home orders, (2) labour availability in the agri-food sector, due to local quarantine measures and the impact on international migrant labour mobility, as well as direct health impacts on workers, (3) farm system resilience, including the economic viability of smaller farms in adverse circumstances, and (4) agricultural system connectivity, such as arbitrary restrictions on food exports during the crisis, and a longer-term rise in national food sovereignty concerns at the expense of unimpeded international trade.[90] The FAO estimated that COVID-19 could increase the numbers of people experiencing chronic hunger in 2020 by 132 million, in addition to the 690 million people previously identified as food-insecure in 2019,[91] equivalent to more than one in ten of the world population being food-insecure.

In Japan, the first phases of the pandemic impacted agriculture and the food sector in several ways. The structure of domestic food demand was disrupted by the closure of schools (which provide lunches to all elementary and middle-school pupils) and by the decline of domestic tourism, though retail sales in supermarkets rose.[92] The moratorium on foreign arrivals also contributed to a sharp fall in food demand in the hospitality sector, and reduced the agricultural workforce by preventing the return to Japan of so-called foreign technical trainees, the farm workers from low-income countries who fulfil the role in Japan filled by migrant labour in other countries. Around 1900 trainees were believed to be affected.[93]

The Abe administration responded in part by proposing to subsidise sales of luxury wagyū beef for school lunches and in supermarkets. In the view of the former senior MAFF bureaucrat Kazuhito Yamashita, the plan was unnecessary, inappropriate, and likely to be in contravention of WTO regulations.[94] The government also offered subsidies totalling 4.6 billion yen for domestic workers to replace the foreign technical trainees in agricultural production activities.[95]

In terms of imports, there was a significant decline in Japan's imports of U.S. beef and pork as the virus spread in the United States. The total volume of beef and pork imports fell from 60,000 metric tons in April to around 40,000 metric tons in each of the next three months.[96] That sharp reduction may have been related to the temporary closure of virus-affected meat processing facilities, due to the infection of at least 16,000 workers in 239 facilities across 23 states, according to U.S. government figures.[97] However, trade volume volatility following the enactment of lower import tariffs in January 2020 under the U.S.-Japan Trade agreement made it difficult to interpret the primary cause of the decline.

Although the WTO, WHO, and FAO together called for countries to refrain from agricultural export bans, India and Vietnam did limit their rice exports temporarily, while Russia limited wheat exports.[98] However, the largest agricultural exporters including the United States, Canada, and Australia did not implement such policies, and overall Japan did not experience significant supply disruptions. As Yamashita observed, international grain prices are now linked to oil prices via the market for biofuel grains, so the decline in energy demand due to coronavirus countermeasures tempered the potential impacts on food grains.[99] In addition, since 2012 Japan has also participated in the ASEAN Plus Three Emergency Rice Reserve, an arrangement designed to mitigate the effects of shortages like those seen in 2008. As such, no rice shortages were reported.

The agriculture ministry also sought to allay food security concerns with the following message featured in a prominent red box on its homepage:

> As for the food system, there are sufficient quantities of supplies, and the supply system is secure.

> We have secured sufficient quantities of rice and wheat stockpiles. There are no problems such as delays in imports from overseas.[100]

The COVID-19 pandemic's main impact on Japan's agricultural and food supply system may have been as a stress test for current structures. As a truly global phenomenon that impacted production and supply networks within and between all countries simultaneously, the pandemic was the sort of large-scale crisis that could have actualised abstract theoretical concerns about secure food access in Japan. The pandemic did reveal some weak points, such as the growing dependence on foreign migrant labour in domestic agricultural production. Yet the initial evidence suggested that the domestic and international food supply systems were both resilient in the case of Japan, and that despite possible marginal declines in areas such as U.S. beef and pork, overall Japanese consumers did not see significant disruption arising from the impacts of COVID-19.

Agriculture, the food system, and climate change

A more gradual but more consequential crisis for agriculture and the global food system is also in progress, caused by the effects of anthropogenic climate change. In this vicious circle, greenhouse gas emissions lead to pollution, temperature increases, and more extreme weather conditions, which in turn drive soil degradation. Facing higher temperatures and less productive land, farmers turn to more chemically and carbon-intensive production methods, which reinforce the cycle of pollution and climate deterioration (Arora, 2019). Climate change will impact farmers through floods, droughts, changes to crop and livestock viability, new pests, pathogens, and weeds, among other means.[101]

The FAO has calculated that 52% of agricultural land worldwide is already moderately or severely degraded, while almost two billion hectares are severely or irreversibly degraded.[102] As Arora (2019) notes, the FAO also predicts that these trends will lead to significant declines in crop production by 2100, estimating that yields of rice will fall by 20-30%, corn/maize by 20-45%, and wheat by 5-50%. At the same time, the global population could grow from 7.7 billion today to 9.7 billion in 2050 and almost 11 billion by 2100, according to median estimates by the U.N.[103] Falling supply and rising demand will cause price increases, and may drive international migration by climate refugees to food-secure countries.

Given the ongoing decline due to socio-economic factors such as population ageing and land abandonment, climate change may further compound the challenge of sustaining Japan's agricultural production base. As early as the mid-2000s, farmers in all 47 prefectures reported global warming effects on fruit-tree cultivation, and farmers in over 70% of prefectures had seen impacts on rice, such as chalky kernels (Sugiura et al, 2012). The government has recorded growing negative impacts in areas such as rice grain quality, fruit discolouration, shiitake mushroom production, and Pacific saury (*sanma*) fisheries (Ministry of the Environment et al, 2018, 3). The potential threat of new pests was underlined by the appearance of the fall armyworm in summer 2019, an invasive moth species whose larvae cause damage to rice, corn, and other crops. First detected in Kagoshima in southern Japan, by summer 2020 it had been identified in about 30 prefectures, although actual damage had been low.[104]

Moreover, the future impacts of climate change on farming will differ dramatically across the various regions of Japan. According to government projections, relative to production levels in the period 1980-2000, yields of high-quality rice could decline by the 2040s by 10-30% in much of the south-central and western Japan but rise by 20-30% in the north-central and northern regions of Honshū and in Hokkaidō (Ministry of the Environment et al, 2018, 3). By the end of the century, the magnitude of change is predicted to exceed 30% in most regions.

In 2015, the government endorsed a *National Plan for Adaptation to the Impacts of Climate Change*, which seeks to mitigate the impacts on agriculture by encouraging shifts to new crops or more resilient cultivars of existing crops (Ministry of the Environment, 2015). Agricultural research institutes developed heat-resistant rice cultivars such as Genki Tsukushi and Nikomaru, while modifications to the planting and transplanting processes may also be effective.[105] Population decline could also mitigate some of the stress of these changes on the domestic food supply system. The government's median estimates are that Japan's population would decline from 127 million in 2017 to 111 million in 2040, 99 million in 2053, and 88 million in 2065,[106] the latter figure representing a potential 30% decrease in calorie-based food demand.

The effects of the climate change crisis will be significantly more consequential than the coronavirus pandemic. It is likely that agricultural yields in much of central and southern Japan will progressively decline by up to one-third in subsequent decades, while those at more northern latitudes could increase by similar amounts. Assuming that lowlands will be affected more than uplands with cooler temperatures, the most productive agricultural land may be affected most significantly, while more marginal upland farms may see relative improvements. Taken together, these cross-cutting effects would amplify existing problems of ageing farmers and land abandonment, and cause significant disruption to agricultural production. Overseas, global warming and population increase will create upward pressure on food demand, which could perhaps reduce the price differential between domestic produce and imports, but also make it harder to source food from overseas in a time of increased competition among buyers. Moreover, if other parts of Asia become less habitable due to global warming, Japan could also become a destination for climate-change refugees, which would in turn impact domestic food demand.

8.3 Operationalising Agricultural Ideas as Policy

Health and food safety

Health and food safety have improved gradually throughout the postwar years. Excluding 1955 (when over 12,000 infants were sickened by arsenic-contaminated infant formula), food poisoning cases fell from around 2000 per year in the 1950s and 1960s to around 1000 annually until the mid-1990s, when data collection methods were changed.[107] Since 1997, Japan has seen a steady decline in the most common kinds of food-borne bacterial infections such as *Vibrio parahaemolyticus* and salmonella, with the exception of campylobacter. This latter bacterium is linked to the consumption of raw or undercooked chicken, which along with raw beef and liver remains an occasional part of food culture in some regions of Japan (Vetchapitak and Misawa, 2019).

The legal framework around food safety has also been strengthened. The 2003 Food Sanitation Act was amended in 2019, with changes including the introduction of the Hazard Analysis Critical Control Point (HACCP) system, an international standard for food distribution. The serving of certain raw meats was also restricted, including beef in 2012 and pork in 2015, although this did not lead to an identifiable reduction *E.coli* infection numbers.[108]

The Fukushima Daiichi Nuclear Power Plant disaster in March 2011 severely impacted the safety reputation of Japanese food globally, due to concerns about pollution from radioactive caesium and other elements. In

2019, the International Atomic Energy Agency reported that the situation in Fukushima remained stable, the government was vigilant and "committed to protecting consumers and trade," monitoring measures were appropriate, and that the food supply system was "controlled effectively by the relevant authorities."[109] According to MAFF data, of the countries that imposed import restrictions following 3/11, 34 had lifted them fully as of May 2020, while 10 (including China, the United States, and the EU) had partially lifted them.[110]

Paradoxically, while Japanese food may be considered less safe overseas due to Fukushima, domestic consumers continue to prefer it for its associations with ideas of health and safety, and radiation contamination is not a major issue. In a 2012 survey one year after Fukushima, 26.1% of respondents to a Cabinet Office survey expressed some concern about food safety in relation to the disaster.[111] However, six years later, when respondents were asked what their major concerns were in relation to food safety, irradiated produce did not feature at all, while imported food was the second-highest concern (40.3%), behind food poisoning (41.7%).[112]

On a statistical level, it is difficult to demonstrate conclusively whether Japanese food truly is safer, but overall there is no reason to believe it is less safe. In terms of operationalising policy to satisfy the consumer preferences for healthy and safe food identified in Chapter 7, the government has made progress in areas such as legislative reform, implementing international standards, and reducing instances of food poisoning. It would be appropriate for future administrations to maintain this approach, to ensure that consumers can continue to have access to health and safe foods.

Food self-sufficiency and food security

Food security and food self-sufficiency are ideas that only become truly meaningful in a time of national crisis. Historically, Japan suffered a number of major famines, including the *Kyoho* famine in the 1730s, the *Temmei* famine in the 1780s, and the *Tempo* famine in the 1830s. Within living memory, millions of Japanese civilians experienced starvation due to the Allied naval blockade on food imports and were able to subsist only via a thriving black market (Wright, 2010), before enduring further food shortages after the war. Even in modern peacetime, Japan has experienced occasional disruption to food imports, such as when the United States banned soy bean exports in 1973 in order to prioritise its domestic animal feed supply, or less consequentially following the 2008 rice export ban by

India that caused prices in Japan to rise.[113] Such historical experiences may help explain the ongoing degree of concern with the idea of food self-sufficiency.

Achieving food self-sufficiency and food security as it is understood in Japan requires strengthening the agricultural production base, including farmers and land. The basic structure of the farming sector continued to weaken during the Abe premiership. According to the MAFF's *2020 Plan for Food, Agriculture, and Rural Villages*, the amount of agricultural land declined under Abe by around 140,000 hectares to 4.40 million hectares, double the decline that had been forecast in 2014, and the ministry now expects the agricultural base to decline further to 4.20 million hectares by 2025.[114] The food self-sufficiency rate also fell under Abe from 39% to 37%, underlining the ineffectiveness of the current agricultural policy regime on its own terms. As Yamashita notes, these declines may actually be helpful for those who use the idea of food self-sufficiency cynically and strategically for political purposes, as a lower rate helps "solicit public support for the protection of Japan's agriculture."[115]

In ideational terms, the failure to achieve greater domestic food production stems from the conflict between the national-security dimension of the idea of food self-sufficiency and its strategic political utilisation—which is also a useful example of the exogenous versus endogenous roles of ideas in political economy. Just as a nation's peacetime industrial production structure is only partially related to its wartime capacity, so too is the food self-sufficiency rate in normal times but a loose correlate of food production capacity in a time of national crisis. During such a period, agricultural production patterns would shift, the structure of food consumption would moderate towards more a basic diet, and overall demand would fall due to a reduction in food wastage, all of which would drive up the food self-sufficiency rate significantly.

Public policy that truly aimed at ensuring Japan's food security and self-sufficiency would focus on developing a detailed national plan to reorganise the food production sector in a time of crisis, such as by repurposing parks, golf courses, and sports fields for agricultural purposes. It would help develop vehicles that run on renewable energy sources, so that tractors could continue to plough fields and trucks could ship produce to consumers without imported fuel, and make other arrangements to temporarily replace imported feeds and fertilisers. Finally, it would foster a truly competitive export sector including in rice production, so that items produced for export in normal times could be used domestically in a crisis.

The environment

High environmental pollution levels in the 1950s and 1960s led to the emergence or general recognition of the 'Four Great Pollution-related Diseases' (*Yon Daikōgai-byō*) that damaged public health, the natural environment, and the food chain, including cadmium poisoning (*itai-itai byō*) in Toyama prefecture, methylmercury poisoning (*Minamata-byō)* in Kagoshima and Niigata prefectures, and sulphur dioxide poisoning in Mie prefecture. A series of laws subsequently dealt with such pollution, including the Basic Act for Environmental Pollution Control (1967), the Water Pollution Control Act (1971), and the Basic Environment Act (1993).

In terms of combatting climate change to protect the environment, Japan was an early leader in implementing energy-efficiency improvements following the disruptions of the 1970s oil crises and acted as host of the third Conference of Parties (COP3) meeting in 1997 that saw the agreement of the Kyoto Protocol, but these early successes made it difficult to meet later standards for further marginal improvement (Kawashima, 2001). Japan subsequently became more reluctant in international negotiations, and as the government shifted from nuclear power generation to greater fossil fuel dependency after the 2011 disaster, Japan retreated further from its active role in international climate change action (Kameyama, 2017).

Kameyama (2017) has argued that the Japanese government's approach to climate change since the 1980s was to characterise it as an economic and energy issue. Going forward, to satisfy consumer preferences on the environment and agriculture, government policy should aim at an approach that integrates broader ideas about societal wellbeing. Climate change will alter the relative productive capacity of various regions of Japan and the world, and global warming is likely to drive population shifts across the Japanese archipelago and internationally. Given that about 70% of the topography of Japan is forests, mountains, or waterways, climate change could further reduce the habitable land area of the country. In such circumstances, policies that protect both rural and urban environments and maintain habitable land area will become increasingly important.

Culture and tradition

The maintenance of the role of agricultural communities in preserving national culture and tradition is interlinked with success in the other areas described above, namely in securing a clean environment and a stable agricultural land base that can produce safe and healthy food and preserve the domestic food supply. The effects of demographic ageing are more severe in rural areas, as evidenced by the problem of over eight million abandoned homes (*akiya*), located mostly in rural areas. The limited success of the 'akiya bank' programmes to find new owners for empty homes underscores the fact that new residents are unlikely to move to rural areas without the availability of employment opportunities.[116]

Preserving the culture and traditions of rural areas in Japan, symbolised by satoyama-no-fūkei, will require sustaining an agricultural sector that is economically viable and supported by a range of socio-economic infrastructure to make rural living comfortable. While this remains a complex and difficult goal to achieve, developments in information technology and the increased prevalence of remote working precipitated by the coronavirus pandemic may make rural living more viable in future, helping preserve the culture and tradition of these areas.

8.4 Conclusion

This book has advanced the positive argument that ideas are an essential explanatory variable in the political economy of agriculture in Japan, despite having been largely overlooked in existing academic literatures. Through a study of the historical origins and development of ideas about agriculture, and their articulation and influence in the media and public opinion, the book has presented a range of evidence to support the assertion that exploring the role of ideas is fundamental to a more complete understanding of a sector whose political, cultural, historical, and even philosophical importance far outweighs its modest share of the national economy.

And yet, this positive argument inevitably gives rise to normative conclusions. If ideas about agriculture *are* important variables in the political economy of Japan, then scholars and others *should* take them more seriously when analysing policy debates or international negotiations or various aspects of agriculture and agricultural trade. In particular, and in conclusion, the findings of this study have implications in three areas.

First, for scholars of political economy and related fields of social science, these findings demonstrate the value of taking ideas seriously as exogenous variables with inherent meaning, rather than simply as endogenous variables that are used instrumentally and cynically. Certainly, ideas *can* be used in this latter way, but the case of Japanese agriculture demonstrates there is much value in understanding their separate function as exogenous variables, which can logically or conceptually enable policy preferences because they have inherent meaning for individuals or policy actors.

This in turn opens the way for a reconsideration of the role of material interests in political economy, since material interests can be classified and analysed as simply one type of idea. Rational choice theorists, historical institutionalists, constructivists, and other scholars will adopt different positions on the ontological question of the nature and degree of distinction between material interests and non-material ideas. Yet in a Japanese context that distinction may be harder to maintain, in the sense that the philosophical world view of Japanese Buddhism, as articulated by Dōgen and others, is one of analytical duality—namely that distinctions between things in the world are simply mental constructs rather than reflections of reality.

Second, at the level of domestic politics, the preferences identified in this study deserve greater attention in policy debates. If health and food safety, food self-sufficiency, and environmental concerns are the values that predominate among an enduring majority of voters and consumers, then it is logical that government policy should aim to prioritise and actualise these goals to some greater or lesser extent. In terms of the central issue of maintaining Japan's domestic agricultural production base, acknowledging the distinction between the national security meaning of food self-sufficiency as an exogenous idea and the endogenous way that that same idea gets used strategically to advanced sectional political interests may be a useful step towards resolving the multi-generational concern about how best to supply food for the nation.

Third, at the level of international relations, it is worth re-emphasising how the non-economic values evidenced in this study have roots that go deeply into Japan's past, and how many agrarian ideas speak to basic conceptions of national identity that are still evident today, as when the emperor each year plants a small rice field in the garden of the Imperial Palace in Tokyo in a ceremony that echoes back through centuries of tradition and culture. In the arena of international trade negotiations and globalised food supply networks, such historically deep ideas are now in a battle with neoclassical or neoliberal ideas of free trade, deregulation, corporatisation, and ultimately a greater homogenisation of consumption and culture across the world.

Though market-focused ideas have come to predominate in international politics in recent decades, some years from now scholars may look back on this period as a time when neoliberalism steamrollered most of the global political economy before it, yet somehow a dwindling band of elderly Japanese rice-farmers, supported by voters and consumers who prioritised non-economic concerns, held firm as an outpost of traditional values and ideas that spoke to an older, deeper conception of human and societal flourishing and collective wellbeing. The plot of Kurosawa Akira's classic film *Seven Samurai* is that the farming inhabitants of a remote village are able, through effort and wiles (and the help of some outside allies), to stave off wave after wave of attack from a large and better-armed band of marauding professional brigands, and ultimately to emerge victorious. As an analogue for how some may see the battle of ideas around agriculture in Japan, it may not be entirely inappropriate.

APPENDIX I

TABLE A1: FRAMING CATEGORIES, KEYWORDS, AND EXAMPLE SENTENCES FROM CHAPTER 6

01 ECB (ECONOMIC & BUSINESS): this frame portrays agriculture as being the same as other sectors in the economy, in terms of its role as a business enterprise for those engaged in it and its place as a 'normal' sector of the economy. This frame is consistent with orienting the agricultural sector along market-based lines.

Sample sentence: "In the modern age where the population's income has increased and its diet has improved, the Japanese agriculture sector must wake up to the fact that the time will soon come when it will have to implement diverse management strategies and learn how to make a profit." - Yomiuri, March 19, 1961.

02 SOC (SOCIETAL WELLBEING): portrays agriculture in terms of the wellbeing of society and groups of individuals that make up society, with particular focus on those in challenging circumstances.

Sample sentence: "The complex issues that affect how the government decides on the price of rice are no different this year to any other. However, the decision is made all the more difficult by the fact that this is the first year of the "Income Doubling Plan", and that this decision is the first important, concrete move since the implementation of the Agricultural Basic Law. The rise in the price of goods and wages are good enough reasons alone for raising the price of rice, but the government's desire to correct the wage gap between agriculture and other sectors add yet another reason for a large-scale price hike." - Asahi, June 15, 1961.

03 ENV (ENVIRONMENT): portrays agriculture in terms of its role in maintaining the natural environment and ecosystems, such as fields, mountains, forests, waterways, and wildlife.

Sample sentence: "However, the market principle is not a panacea. By only leaving it to the market, the environment and ecology would be broken, everything would be lost. While talking about "sustainable development"... we should emphasise the importance of protecting a bountiful natural ecology that enables habitats for many kinds of animals." - Asahi, April 21, 1999.

04 NSC (NATIONAL SECURITY): portrays agriculture in terms of its role in achieving aspects of national security, namely those issues which may be considered important for the survival of the nation and the state, like a secure national food supply.

Sample sentence: "Japan's food self-sufficiency rate is declining year by year. Looked at on a supply calorie basis, the food self-sufficiency rate went from 73% in 1965 to 41% in 1997. Grain, which is a basic foodstuff, also fell during this period from 62% to 28%, 135th place out of the 178 countries and regions in the world. The crop self-sufficiency rate for all countries with populations of over 100 million is over 80%. When you consider that the international crop trade is made up of countries trading the limited surplus of crops that are left over once they have met their own domestic demand, it is fair to say that the situation is harsh." - Mainichi, April 17, 1999.

05 CTN (CULTURE & TRADITION): portrays agriculture in terms of its cultural, historical, and/or religious significance, and its role in contemporary society.

Sample sentence: "Agriculture's role is, not only food production, but protecting the land, environment, scenery, and traditional culture. That should be emphasised more." - Asahi, September 18, 1996.

06 HFS (HEALTH & FOOD SAFETY): portrays agriculture in terms of the contribution of agricultural products to health and nutrition, such as providing 'safe 'food, food of high quality etc.

Sample sentence: "The new agricultural basic law lists supplying safe, good-quality food at a reasonable price, and more properly labelling food items. That is one of the directions at which agricultural policy should naturally aim." - Yomiuri, March 10, 1999.

07 GOV (GOVERNMENT INTERVENTION): portrays agriculture as an area in which government intervention to help or support farmers is appropriate, such as through financial support or other measures.

Sample sentence: "It may not be a popular decision, but we need to devote support funds to developing a new agricultural system. We don't care if we devote more money to this goal than the total debt of the Food Control System. The very reason governments collect money from taxpayers is so that they can use it to make reforms such as these." - Yomiuri, July 18, 1961.

08 MKT (MARKET): portrays agriculture as an appropriate area for utilising or expanding market-oriented policies or a laissez-faire approach by the government.

Sample sentence: "To rid itself of these problems and refresh the rice pricing system, the government's best bet is to completely dismantle the system and turn the supply and demand of rice over to market principles." - Yomiuri, June 14, 1961.

09 MFN (MULTIFUNCTIONALITY): portrays agriculture as having a multiplicity of functions that it may perform in relation to the economy, society and especially the environment. By definition, this is a 'meta-frame ' that incorporates several other frames, but it may be identified by name or by listing in close proximity a range of functions performed.

Sample sentence: "The outlook for the 21st century is that the role for agriculture and forestry to carry out is not just the supply of safe food. It should positively contribute to the preservation of land and environment. Without the continued operation of agricultural production, the bountiful natural environment of agricultural and mountain villages can't be protected."- Asahi, August 28, 1998.

10 TRD (TRADE ISSUE): portrays agriculture in terms of its role as an issue in trade and international affairs such as imports, exports and trade agreement negotiations.

Sample sentence: "The government, the LDP, and the National Agricultural Cooperatives Federation [JA-Zenchū] have decided from April next year to move to the tariffication of rice imports. Imports that exceed the "Minimum Access" (minimum import obligation quantity) will become freely importable if they pay the tariff. For the time being, there is no prospect of an increase of imports that can be protected by high tariff rates, but one of these days, the tariffs will come down. To prepare them for future tariff lowering, the government must strengthen the legs of rice farmers." - Nikkei, December 19, 1998.

11 POL (POLITICAL ISSUE): portrays agriculture in terms of its importance as a domestic political issue, in relation to political parties and other major political actors.

Sample sentence: "It is a crucial moment as to whether or not we can break out of the "pork-barrel style" agricultural policy that continued after the war." - Yomiuri, September 20, 1998.

APPENDIX II

TABLE A2: CABINET OFFICE PUBLIC OPINION SURVEYS ON AGRICULTURE AND FOOD

Year	Japanese Title	Translation	Sample size	Link
2014 (HEISEI 26)	Nōsangyoson ni kan suru seron chōsa	Public Opinion Survey on Agricultural, Mountainous and Fishing Villages	1880	http://survey.gov-online.go.jp/h26/h26-nousan/index.html
2009 (HEISEI 20)	Shokuryō, nōgyō, nōson no yakuwari ni kan suru seron chōsa	Public Opinion Survey on the Roles of Food, Agriculture and Agricultural Villages	3144	http://survey.gov-online.go.jp/h20/h20-shokuryou/index.html
2007 (HEISEI 18)	Shokuryō no kyōkyū ni kan suru tokubetsu seron chōsa	Special Public Opinion Survey on the Food Supply	1727	http://survey.gov-online.go.jp/tokubetu/h18/h18-syokuryo.pdf
2000 (HEISEI 12)	Nōsanbutsu bōeki ni kan suru seron chōsa	Public Opinion Survey on Agricultural Trade	3570	http://survey.gov-online.go.jp/h12/nousan/1.html

Year	Japanese Title	Translation	Sample size	Link
1996 (Heisei 8)	Shokuryō, nōgyō, nōson no yakuwari ni kan suru seron chōsa	Public Opinion Survey on the Roles of Food, Agriculture and Agricultural Villages	3567	http://survey.gov-online.go.jp/h08/food.html
1993 (Heisei 5)	Shokuseikatsu, nōson no yakuwari ni kan suru seron chōsa	Public Opinion Survey on Eating Habits and the Role of Agricultural Villages	2219	http://survey.gov-online.go.jp/h05/H05-11-05-11.html
1990 (Heisei 2)	Shokuseikatsu, nōson no yakuwari ni kan suru seron chōsa	Public Opinion Survey on Eating Habits and the Role of Agricultural Villages	2292	http://survey.gov-online.go.jp/h02/H02-10-02-18.html
1987 (Shōwa 62)	Shokuseikatsu, nōson no yakuwari ni kan suru seron chōsa	Public Opinion Survey on Eating Habits and the Role of Agricultural Villages	2323	http://survey.gov-online.go.jp/s62/S62-09-62-11.html
1984 (Shōwa 59)	Shokuryō oyobi nōgyō, nōson ni kan suru seron chōsa	Public Opinion Survey on Food, Agriculture and Agricultural Villages	4087	http://survey.gov-online.go.jp/s59/S59-09-59-09.html

Year	Japanese Title	Translation	Sample size	Link
1980 (SHŌWA 55)	Shokuseikatsu, shokuryō mondai ni kan suru seron chōsa	Public Opinion Survey on Eating Habits and the Food Provision Problem	2494	http://survey.gov-online.go.jp/s55/S55-09-55-10.html
1978 (SHŌWA 53)	Shokuseikatsu, shokuryō mondai ni kan suru seron chōsa	Public Opinion Survey on Eating Habits and the Food Provision Problem	4075	http://survey.gov-online.go.jp/s53/S53-08-53-06.html
1975 (SHŌWA 50)	Shokuseikatsu oyobi shokuryō ni kan suru seron chōsa	Public Opinion Survey on Eating Habits and Food Provision	4211	http://survey.gov-online.go.jp/s50/S50-08-50-12.html

References

Alesina, Alberto, Guido Cozzi, and Noemi Mantovan. 2012. "The Evolution of Ideology, Fairness and Redistribution". *The Economic Journal* 122 (565): 1244-1261.

Anderson, Kym. 1986. "Economic growth, structural change and the political economy of protection." In *The Political Economy of Agricultural Protection*, edited by Kym Anderson and Yujiro Hayami, 7-16. Sydney: Allen & Unwin.

Anderson, Kym, and Rod Tyers. 1987. "Japan's Agricultural Policy in International Perspective." *Journal of the Japanese and International Economies* 1 (2): 131-46.

Ando, Mitsuyo, & Fukunari Kimura. 2008." Japanese FTA/EPA Strategies and Agricultural Protection." *Keio Business Review* 44: 1-25.

Arora, N.K. 2019. "Impact of climate change on agriculture production and its sustainable solutions." *Environmental Sustainability* 2: 95-96. https://doi.org/10.1007/s42398-019-00078-w

Ashizawa, Kuniko. 2008. "When Identity Matters: State Identity, Regional Institution-Building, and Japanese Foreign Policy." *International Studies Review*, 10 (3): 571-598.

Béland, Daniel, and Robert Henry Cox. 2011. "Introduction". In *Ideas and Politics in Social Science Research*, edited by Daniel Béland and Robert Henry Cox, 3-22. Oxford University Press.

Blyth, Mark. 1997. "Any More Bright Ideas? The Ideational Turn in Comparative Political Economy." *Comparative Politics* 29, no. 2 (January): 229-250.

Brown, Drusilla K., Alan V. Deardorff, and Robert M. Stern. 2003. "Multilateral, Regional, and Bilateral Trade-Policy Options for the United States and Japan." *World Economy* 26 (6): 803-828.

Bull, Tim, and Ivan Roberts. 2001. *Agricultural Trade Policies in Japan: The Need for Reform*. ABARE Research Report 01.5. Canberra.

Bullock, Robert. 1997." *Nokyo*: A Short Cultural History." Japan Policy Research Institute Working Paper No. 41. http://www.jpri.org/publications/workingpapers/wp41.html

Calder, Kent. 1989. *Crisis and Compensation: Public Policy and Political Stability in Japan*. Princeton University Press.

Campbell, John L. 2004. *Institutional Change and Globalization.* Princeton University Press.

Clements, Kenneth, and Jiawei Si. 2018. "Engel's Law, Diet Diversity and the Quality of Food Consumption." *American Journal of Agricultural Economics* 100, no. 1 (January). https://doi.org/10.1093/ajae/aax053

Coleman, William D., Grace D. Skogstad and Michael M. Atkinson. 1996. "Paradigm shifts and Policy Networks: Cumulative Change in Agriculture." *Journal of Public Policy* 16 (3): 273-301.

Cortell, Andrew P., and James W. Davis. 2005. "When norms clash: international norms, domestic practices, and Japan's internalisation of the GATT/WTO". *Review of International Studies* 31 (1): 3-25.

Crawcour, Sydney. 1989. "Economic change in the nineteenth century." In *The Cambridge History of Japan, Volume 5: the Nineteenth Century*, edited by Marius Jansen, 385-450. Cambridge University Press.

Cwiertka, Katarzyna. 2007. *Modern Japanese Cuisine: Food, Power, and National Identity*. Reaktion Books.

Danbom, David B. 1991. "Romantic Agrarianism in Twentieth-Century America." *Agricultural History* 65 (4): 1-12.

de Bary, Wm. Theodore, Carol Gluck, et al (eds). 2010. *Sources of Japanese Tradition: 1600 to 2000.* Columbia University Press. *Amazon Kindle edition.*

DellaVigna, Stefano, and Ethan Kaplan. 2007. "The Fox News Effect: Media Bias and Voting." *The Quarterly Journal of Economics* 122 (3): 1187-1234.

Dearing, James W., & Everett M. Rogers. 1996. *Agenda Setting*. Sage.

Dore, Ronald P. 1986. *Flexible Rigidities: Industrial Policy and Structural Adjustment in Japan, 1970-1980*. Stanford University Press.

Dower, John W. 1999. *Embracing Defeat: Japan in the Wake of World War II*. New York: Norton.

Downs, Anthony. 1957. *An Economic Theory of Democracy*. New York: Harper & Row.

Dyck, John. 1998. "U.S.-Japan Agreements on Beef Imports: A Case of Successful Bilateral Negotiations". In *Regional Trade Agreements and U.S. Agriculture: Agricultural Economic Report No.771*, edited by Mary E. Burfisher and Elizabeth A. Jones, Chapter 9. Economic Research Service, U.S. Department of Agriculture.

East Asia Analytical Unit. 1997. *A New Japan? Change in Asia's Megamarket*. Australia: Department of Foreign Affairs and Trade.

Entman, Robert M. 1993. "Framing: Toward Clarification of a Fractured Paradigm". *Journal of Communication* 43 (4): 51–58.

Estevez-Abe, Margarita. 2008. *Welfare and Capitalism in postwar Japan: Party, Bureaucracy, and Business.* Cambridge University Press.

Flath, David. 2000. *The Japanese Economy*. Oxford University Press.

Francks, Penelope. 1999. *Japanese Economic Development: Theory and Practice*. Routledge: London and New York.

Freiner, Nicole. 2017. *Rice and Agricultural Policies in Japan: the Loss of a Traditional Lifestyle*. Palgrave MacMillan.

Fujiki, Hiroshi. 2000. "Japanese Rice Market Liberalization: A Competitive Equilibrium Approach". *Japanese Economic Review* 51 (4): 492-518.

Fukui, Haruhiko. 1975. "The Japanese Farmer and Politics." In *The Japanese Economy in International Perspective*, edited by Isaiah Frank, 134-167. Baltimore: Johns Hopkins University Press.

Gluck, Carol. 1987. *Japan's Modern Myths: Ideology in the Late Meiji Period.* Princeton University Press.

Gofas, Andreas, and Colin Hay. 2010. "Varieties of ideational explanations." In *The Role of Ideas in Political Analysis: A Portrait of Contemporary Debates*, edited by Andreas Gofas and Colin Hay, 13-55. Routledge.

Goldstein, Judith. 1989. "The impact of ideas on trade policy: the origins of U.S. agricultural and manufacturing policies". *International Organisation* 43 (1): 31-71.

Goldstein, Judith, and Robert Keohane. 1993. *Ideas and Foreign Policy: Beliefs, Institutions, and Political Change*. Cornell University Press.

Hall, Peter A. 1993. "Policy Paradigms, Social Learning, and the State: the Case of Economic Policymaking in Britain." *Comparative Politics* 25 (3): 275-296.

Hausman, Daniel M. and Michael S. McPherson. 2006. *Economic Analysis, Moral Philosophy and Public Policy*. Cambridge University Press.

Havens, Thomas R. H. 1974. *Farm and Nation in Modern Japan: Agrarian Nationalism, 1870-1940*. Princeton University Press.

Hayami, Yujiro. 1988. *Japanese Agriculture Under Siege: the Political Economy of Agricultural Policies*. Macmillan Press.

Honma, Masayoshi. 2015. "The TPP and Agricultural Reform in Japan." In *The Political Economy of Japanese Trade* Policy, edited by Aurelia George Mulgan and Masayoshi Honma, 94-122. Palgrave Macmillan.

Ichioka, Osama, and Toshiaki Tachibanaki. 1989." General Equilibrium Evaluations of Tariffs, Nontariff Barriers and Subsidies for Agriculture in Japan." *Economics Studies Quarterly* 40 (4): 317-335.

Itoh, Mayumi. 1994. "Kome Kaikoku and Japanese Internationalization." *Asian Survey* 34 (11): 991-1001.

JA Zenchū. 2020. "Multifunctionality of Agriculture in Japan." http://www.zenchu-ja.or.jp/eng/multi_functionality

Japan Customs. 2020. "Japan's Tariff Schedule (Statistical Code for Import." https://www.customs.go.jp/english/tariff/index.htm.

Kasai, Hideo. 2015. "Food Safety Measures in Japan." *Japan Medical Association Journal* 58 (4): 170-173.

Katz, Richard (2014). *The Cost of Japan's Farm Protectionism, Part III.* New York: Japan Watchers LLC.

Katzenstein, Peter. 1996. *Cultural Norms and National Security: Police and Military in Postwar Japan*. Ithaca: Cornell University Press.

Kawai, Masahiro, and Ganeshan Wignaraja. 2007. "ASEAN+3 or ASEAN+6: Which Way Forward?" ADB Institute Discussion Paper No. 77. http://www.wto.org/english/tratop_e/region_e/con_sep07_e/kawai_wignaraja_e.pdf.

Kameyama, Yasuko. 2017. *Climate Change Policy in Japan: From the 1980s to 2015*. London: Routledge.

Kawashima, Yasuko. 2001. "Japan and Climate Change: Responses and Explanations." *Energy & Environment* 12 (2–3): 167–179. https://doi.org/10.1260/0958305011500689

Kosai, Yutaka. 1989. "The Japanese Economy, 1945-1973.". In *Cambridge History of Japan, Volume 6: the Twentieth* Century, edited by Peter Duus, 494-537. Cambridge University Press.

Lasswell, Harold D. 1950. *National Security and Individual Freedom*. New York: McGraw-Hill.

Lee, Hiro, and Ken Itakura. 2014. "TPP, RCEP, and Japan's Agricultural Policy Reform." OSIPP Discussion Paper No 14E003, Osaka University.
http://www.osipp.osaka-u.ac.jp/archives/DP/2014/DP2014E003.pdf

Lee, Hiro, and Dominique van der Mensbrugghe. 2008. "Regional Integration, Sectoral Adjustments and Natural Groupings in East Asia." *International Journal of Applied Economics* 5 (2): 57-79.

Mansfield, Edward D., and Diana C. Mutz. 2009. "Support for Free Trade: self-interest, sociotropic politics, and out-group anxiety." *International Organization*, 63 (3): 425-57.

Mayda, Ana Maria, and Dani Rodrik. 2005. "Why are some people (and countries) more protectionist than others?" *European Economic Review* 49, no. 6 (August): 1393-1430.

McCombs, Maxwell. 2004. *Setting the Agenda: The Mass Media and Public Opinion*. Cambridge: Polity Press.

Midford, Paul. 2011. *Rethinking Japanese Public Opinion and Security.* California: Stanford University Press.

Ministry of the Environment. 2015. "National Plan for Adaptation to the Impacts of Climate Change." https://www.env.go.jp/en/focus/docs/files/20151127-101.pdf.

Ministry of the Environment at al. 2018). "Climate Change in Japan and its Impacts: Synthesis Report on Observations, Projections and Impact assessments of Climate Change, 2018". https://www.env.go.jp/earth/tekiou/pamph2018_full_Eng.pdf.

Mosk, Carl. 2008. *Japanese Economic Development: Markets, norms, structures*. Routledge: London and New York.

Mulgan, Aurelia George. 2000. *The Politics of Japanese Agriculture*. London and New York: Routledge.

Mulgan, Aurelia George. 2005. *Japan's Interventionist State: the role of MAFF*. Routledge Curzon.

Mulgan, Aurelia George. 2006. *Japan's Agricultural Policy Regime.* Routledge: London and New York.

Mulgan, Aurelia George. 2014. "Agriculture". In *The SAGE Handbook of Modern Japan Studies, edited by* James D. Babb, 583-602. Sage.

Mulgan, Aurelia George. 2011. "The Farm Lobby". In *Japanese Politics Today: From Karaoke to Kabuki Democracy,* edited by Takeshi Inoguchi and Purnendra Jain, 109-126. Palgrave Macmillan.

Mulgan, Aurelia George. 2015. "Understanding Japanese Trade Policy: A Political Economy Perspective". In *The Political Economy of Japanese Trade* Policy, edited by Aurelia George Mulgan and Masayoshi Honma, 1-40. Palgrave Macmillan.

Mulgan, Aurelia George. 2016. "Much Ado About Something? The Abe Government's Reform of Japan's Agricultural Cooperatives (JA)." *Japan Studies* 36 (1): 83-103.

Mulgan, Aurelia George. 2018. *The Abe Administration and the Rise of the Prime Ministerial Executive*. Routledge.

Najita, Tetsuo, and H. D. Harootunian. 1998. "Japan's Revolt Against the West". In *Modern Japanese Thought,* edited by Bob Tadashi Wakabayashi, 202-272. Cambridge University Press.

Nakano, Takeshi. 2009. *Amakudari to wa Nanika* [What is 'Amakudari'?]. Tokyo: Kōdansha.

North, Douglass C. 2006. "What is Missing from Political Economy?" In *The Oxford Handbook of Political Economy,* edited by Barry R. Weingast and Donald A. Wittman, 1003-1009. Oxford University Press.

OECD. 2009. *Evaluation of Agricultural Policy Reforms in Japan*. OECD. http://www.oecd.org/japan/42791674.pdf.

OECD. 2010. *Producer and Consumer Support Estimates OECD Database, 1986-2003: User's Guide*. OECD.

http://www.oecd.org/tad/32361345.pdf
OECD. 2013. *OECD Economic Surveys: Japan 2013*. OECD. http://www.oecd.org/eco/surveys/Overview%20Japan%202013%20English.pdf

Ogura, Takekazu. 2000. *Agricultural Developments in Modern Japan: Japanese Economic History 1930-1960, Volume VI*. Routledge: London and New York.

Ogura, Takekazu. 1980. *Can Japanese Agriculture Survive? A Historical and Comparative Approach*. Tokyo: Agricultural Policy Research Center.

Ohnuki-Tierney, Emiko. 1989. *Rice As Self: Japanese Identities Through Time*. Princeton University Press.

Ozawa, Takeshi. 2017. "Agricultural land use policy in Japan in an era of declining population." *Wildlife and Human Society* 5 (1): 17-27.

Petri, Peter, Michael G. Plummer and Fan Zhai. 2011." The Trans-Pacific Partnership and Asia-Pacific Integration: A Quantitative Assessment." *East-West Center Working Papers, Economic Series*, 119. http://www.eastwestcenter.org/sites/default/files/private/econwp119_2.pdf

Petri, Peter, and Michael Plummer. 2011. "The Economic Effects of the Trans-Pacific Partnership: New Estimates." Peterson Institute of International Economics Working Paper WP 16-2. https://www.piie.com/publications/wp/wp16-2.pdf

Piermartini, Roberta, and Robert Teh. 2005. "Demystifying Modelling Methods for Trade Policy." *WTO Discussion Paper, No. 10*. www.wto.org/English/res_e/booksp_e/discussion_papers10_e.pdf

Pyle, Kenneth. 1998." Meiji Conservatism". In *Modern Japanese Thought*, edited by Bob Tadashi Wakabayashi, 98-146. Cambridge University Press.

Ramseyer, J. Mark, and Frances McCall Rosenbluth. 1993. *Japan's Political Marketplace*. Cambridge: Harvard University Press.

Ramseyer, J. Mark, & Frances McCall Rosenbluth. 1995. *The Politics of Oligarchy: Institutional Choice in Imperial Japan*. Cambridge University Press.

Ravenhill, John. 2001. *APEC and the Construction of Pacific Rim Regionalism*. Cambridge.

Regan, D. E. 1978 "Rationality in Policy-Making: Two Concepts Not One". *Long Range Planning* 11 (5): 83-88. https://doi.org/10.1016/0024-6301(78)90034-1

Rodrik, Dani. 2014. "When Ideas Trump Interests: Preferences, Worldviews, and Policy Innovations". *Journal of Economic Perspectives* 28 (1): 189–208.

Mukand, Sharun, and Dani Rodrik. 2018. "The Political Economy of Ideas: On Ideas Versus Interests in Policymaking." NBER Working Papers, No. 24467. https://www.nber.org/papers/w24467

Roningen,Vernon O., and Praveen M. Dixit. 1991." Reforming Agricultural Policies: the Case of Japan". *Journal of Asian Economics* 2 (1): 87-111.

Ruggie, John Gerard. 1998. "What Makes the World Hang Together? Neo-Utilitarianism and the Social Constructivist Challenge". *International Organisation* 52 (4): 855-885.

Sakuyama, Takumi. 2010. "Determinants of Tariff Dependence in Japan's Agricultural Protection: An Empirical Investigation Using Panel-Data." *Studies in Regional Science* 40 (3): 679-694.

Sasada Hironori. 2010. "Japan's New Agricultural Trade Policy and Electoral Reform: 'Agricultural Policy in an Offensive Posture [*seme no nosei*]'." *Japanese Journal of Political Science* 9 (2): 121-144.

Scheiner, Ethan. 2005. *Democracy Without Competition in Japan: Opposition Failure in a One-Party Dominant State*. New York: Cambridge University Press.

Sheingate, Adam D. 2000. "Institutions and Interest Group Power: Agricultural Policy in the United States, France, and Japan." *Studies in American Political Development* 14 (2): 184-211.

Sheingate, Adam D. 2001. *The Rise of the Agricultural Welfare State: Institutions and Interest Group Power in the United States, France, and Japan*. Princeton: Princeton University Press.

Shepsle, Kenneth. 1985. "Comment". In *Regulatory Policy and the Social Sciences,* edited by Roger G. Noll, 231-37. Berkley: California University Press.

Skogstad, Grace. 1998. "Ideas, Paradigms and Institutions: Agricultural Exceptionalism in the European Union and the United States." *Governance* 11 (4): 436-490.

Solis, Mireya. 2017. *Dilemmas of a Trading Nation: Japan and the United States in the Evolving Asia-Pacific Order*. Washington, D.C.: Brookings Institution Press.

Statistics Bureau of Japan. 2019. *Statistical Handbook of Japan*. https://www.stat.go.jp/english/data/handbook/pdf/2019all.pdf

Sugihara, Kaoru. 1996." Agriculture and Industrialization: the Japanese experience". In *The Nature of Industrialization, Volume 4, Agriculture and Industrialization: from the Eighteenth Century to the Present Day,* edited by Peter Mathias and John A. Davis. Wiley-Blackwell.

Sugiura, Toshihiko, et al. 2012. "Overview of Recent Effects of Global Warming on Agricultural Production in Japan." *Japan Agricultural Research Quarterly* 46 (1): 7-13.

Suzuki-Morris, Tessa. 1989. *A History of Japanese Economic Thought.* Routledge: London and New York.

Thies, Michael F. 1998. "When Will Pork Leave the Farm? Institutional Bias in Japan and the United States." *Legislative Studies Quarterly* 23 (4): 467-492.

Tsuzuki, Chushichi. 2005. *The Pursuit of Power in Modern Japan, 1825-1995*. Oxford University Press.

Urata, Shujiro. 2007." Japan's FTA Strategy and a Free Trade Area of Asia Pacific". In *An APEC Trade Agenda? The Political Economy of a Free Trade Area of the Asia Pacific.* Pacific Economic Cooperation Council. https://www.pecc.org/resources/trade-and-investment-1/2038-japans-fta-strategy-and-free-trade-area-of-asia-pacific-ftaap/file

Urata, Shujiro. 2015. "Postwar Japanese Trade Policy". In *The Political Economy of Japanese Trade* Policy, Aurelia George Mulgan and Masayoshi Honma, 41-70. Palgrave Macmillan.

Valaskivi, Katja. 2007. "Mapping Media and Communication Research: Japan." *University of Helsinki Department of Communication, Research Reports 4/2007*. http://www.helsinki.fi/crc/Julkaisut/ReportJapan.pdf

Valaskivi, Katja. 2014. "Mass Media in Japan". In *The SAGE Handbook of Modern Japan Studies*, edited by James D. Babb, 63-79. Sage.

Vetchapitak, Torrung, and Naoaki Misawa. 2019."Current Status of *Campylobacter* Food Poisoning in Japan." *Food Safety* 7 (3): 61-73. https://doi.org/10.14252/foodsafetyfscj.D-19-00001

Vlastos, Stephen. 1998. "Agrarianism Without Tradition: the Radical Critique of Prewar Japanese Modernity". In *Mirror of Modernity: Invented Traditions of Modern Japan,* edited by Stephen Vlastos, 79-94. Berkeley: University of California Press.

Vogel, Steven K. 1999. "When interests are not preferences: the cautionary tale of Japanese consumers". *Comparative Politics* 31 (2): 187-207.

Waswo, Ann. 1989." The transformation of rural society, 1900-1950". In *Cambridge History of Japan*, *Volume 6: the Twentieth Century,* edited by Peter Duus, 541-605. Cambridge University Press.

Weaver, David H. 2007. "Thoughts on Agenda Setting, Framing, and Priming." *Journal of Communication* 57: 142-147.

Wendt, Alexander. 1992. "Anarchy is what states make of it: the social construction of power politics". *International Organization* 46 (2): 391-425.

Wendt, Alexander. 1999. *Social Theory of International Relations*. Cambridge: Cambridge University Press.
World Bank. 2020. "Urban Population (% of total population)—Japan.". https://data.worldbank.org/indicator/SP.URB.TOTL.IN.ZS?locations=JP
Wright, Michael. 2010. "In Search of 'Silver Rice': Starvation and Deprivation in Work War II-era Japan". *Studies on Asia*, Series IV, 1 (1).
Yamashita, Kazuhito. 2014. *Nōkyō Kaitai: The Road to Dissolution of JA*. Tokyo: Takarajimasha.
Yamashita, Kazuhito. 2015. "Japanese Agricultural Trade Negotiations". In *The Political Economy of Japanese Trade* Policy, edited by Aurelia George Mulgan and Masayoshi Honma, 71-93. Palgrave Macmillan.
Yoshimatsu, Hidetaka. 2005. "Japan's Keidanren and Free Trade Agreements: Societal Interests and Trade Policy". *Asian Survey* 49 (2): 258-278.

NOTES

[1] "Japanese eat more meat, fewer vegetables than decade ago: official data," *The Japan Times*, December 7, 2012.
https://www.japantimes.co.jp/news/2012/12/07/national/japanese-eat-more-meat-fewer-vegetables-than-decade-ago-official-data/

[2] The 2014 Japan-Australia Economic Partnership Agreement (JAEPA) was Japan's first agreement with a major agriculture-producing nation, and included around 50% tariff reductions on beef imports as well as provisions for cheese and wine. For details, see Honma (2015, 99-101).

[3] Structural change is defined, after Dore (1986, 29), as "changes in composition of outputs between major activities (/sectors), composition of output within manufacturing, the role of trade in the economy and the composition of imports and exports, composition of the labour force and its sectoral distribution, the organisational and control structures of business enterprises, the distribution of income, the mechanisms and coefficients of factors underlying growth rates, such as savings, investments, technological innovation and demand creation."

[4] This literature overlaps with more general historical institutionalist studies that explain the persistence of agriculture's privileged position in terms of the strong links between peak associations of farmers and farm groups. See, for example, Sheingate (2000).

[5] Other possible translations include 'sanctuary items,' 'holy ground,' or 'sacred cows.'

[6] Typically, national security refers to military aspects of the security of the nation, and frequently also encompasses political, economic, environmental, and, latterly, cybersecurity aspects. A classic definition of national security by Lasswell (1950, 51) is pertinent for the sense in which it is used in the present study: "The distinctive meaning of national security means freedom from foreign dictation." In this light, food self-sufficiency can certainly be considered an issue of national security, as it seems to have been viewed in Japan both historically and in contemporary society.

[7] A fuller discussion and definition of non-economic concerns is given in Chapter 3 Section 3.

[8] In the text (apart from the foreword), Japanese names are given in the Japanese convention.

[9] "Heisei 31 nendo Nōrinsuisanshō kankei yosan no kosshi" [Outline of MAFF Budget for 2019], MAFF. https://www.maff.go.jp/j/budget/attach/pdf/31kettei-44.pdf.

[10] MAFF, "Outline of MAFF budget for 2019."

[11] "Second MAFF 2020 Supplementary Budget for COVID-19 Response," USDA Report number JA2020-0116, June 1, 2020. https://bit.ly/35wnl5O.

[12] Yamashita Kazuhito, "Japan's farm protection policy untouchable even for PM Abe's office." Canon Institute for Global Studies, February 27, 2020. https://cigs.canon/en/article/20200227_6247.html

[13] Yamashita, "Japan's farm protection policy untouchable."

[14] Specific tariffs are specified per unit of item, such as per kilogram, different from ad valorem (value-based) tariffs.

[15] Harada Yutaka, "Japan's Agriculture and the TPP." *Tokyo Foundation,* November 21, 2013. http://www.tokyofoundation.org/en/articles/2013/japan-agriculture-and-tpp

[16] This latter case is also termed *yokosuberi*, or 'sideslip.'

[17] Yamashita Kazuhito, "For Whom Are the Food/Agricultural Policies? Officials in the 'Agricultural Village' Disregard Stable Supply', *Canon Institute of Global Studies*, April 10, 2020. https://cigs.canon/en/article/20200410_6339.html.

[18] *Japan Times,* "Japanese eat more meat, fewer vegetables than decade ago."

[19] The economic processes captured within CGE models has been usefully summarised as follows: "Trade liberalisation measures including tariff reductions would stimulate trade by lowering prices on tradable goods. This would result in increases in national output of exporting countries, while increasing access to the markets of trading partners. Meanwhile, domestic production resources—land, capital, labor, and intermediate inputs— would be used more efficiently, as domestic distortions, including those due to trade barriers, are reduced. These combined effects— one from foreign markets and the other from the domestic market— are expected to result in the expansion of production and an increase in income and welfare." See Kawasaki Kenichi, "A U.S.-Japan free trade agreement simulation." *Research Institute of Economy, Trade, and Industry*, March 13, 2003. http://www.rieti.go.jp/en/miyakodayori/063.html

[20] "Sangyō Renkanhyō (Kakuhō)" [Confirmed Report of Input-Output Table], *Ministry of Internal Affairs and Communications*, 2015. https://www.soumu.go.jp/toukei_toukatsu/data/io/015index.html

[21] *The 93rd Statistical Yearbook of Ministry of Agriculture, Forestry and Fisheries*, MAFF, Section 4-2-1. https://www.maff.go.jp/e/data/stat/93th/index.html#15

[22] *93rd Statistical Yearbook*, Section 2-1-1.

[23] "The Organisational Structure of the JA Group." JA-Zenchū

[24] MAFF, "Nōrinsuisan Kihon Dēta-shū" [Collected Basic Data for Agriculture, Forestry and Fisheries], https://www.maff.go.jp/j/tokei/sihyo/

[25] MAFF, Collected Basic Data.

[26] "Jigyō sōrieki 0.5% gen, izen teiraku keikō tsuzuku, Heisei 30 nendo sōgō JA kessan" [Operational gross profits down 0.5%, continuing previous downward trend, in JA's overall accounts for 2018], *JAcom*, November 19, 2019. https://www.jacom.or.jp/noukyo/news/2019/11/191108-39596.php.

[27] "Promotion of Domestic Reforms to Thrive in Global Competition," Keidanren, April 16, 2013.

http://www.keidanren.or.jp/en/policy/2013/034_proposal.html#part6.

[28] Keidanren, "Promotion of Domestic Reforms."

[29] Andrew Chatzky, "Does the New U.S.-Japan Trade Deal Matter?" *Council on Foreign Relations*, October 4, 2019. https://www.cfr.org/in-brief/does-new-us-japan-trade-deal-matter

[30] The phrase deliberately echoed the original *kaikoku*, when Japan was forcibly (re-)opened to the world by Commodore Perry in the 1850s. External political pressure (*gaiatsu*) has often been used strategically by domestic advocates of reform ever since that time.

[31] "Brazil government denies reports of 2010 mad cow case," Reuters, https://www.reuters.com/article/us-brazil-madcow/brazil-government-denies-reports-of-2010-mad-cow-case-idUSBRE8B60GH20121207.

[32] For example, Scheiner (2005) has argued that Japan's postwar polity reified and perpetuated a system of clientelism (combining patronage and pork-barrel politics) and government that was highly financially centralised. Through this system, LDP candidates prospered in their districts by becoming pipelines to channel central government spending to rural districts, while local opposition party candidates at the local level did poorly, since they lacked access to these financial resources. Voters were also part of this clientelist relationship, since they implicitly saw votes as being units to be exchanged for pork.

[33] In 2011, the highest level of disparity among districts for the lower chamber (the House of Representatives) was 2.52:1, meaning that a voter in the sparsely populated Kochi District Number 3 effectively had 2.52 times the voting power of a voter in the densely populated Chiba District Number 4. During the postwar periods, the disparities have been as high as 4.99 in the lower house (in the early 1970s) and 6.59 in the upper house in 1992. See Tsuchiya Hideo, "Fifty Years On, Japan's High Court Yet to Act on Vote Disparity," *Nippon.com*, December 15, 2014. https://www.nippon.com/en/currents/d00150/

[34] Mulgan (2000, 476) also noted that politicians may opportunistically choose to style themselves as farm representatives for the purpose of widening their support base.

[35] MAFF, *93rd Statistical Yearbook*.

[36] Preferences are complete when they rank all the alternatives faced by an agent. They are transitive when, if x is preferred to y and y is preferred to z, x is also preferred to z.

[37] The essay appeared in English in both the *Christian Science Monitor* and the *New York Times*. It was an adapted translation of an essay entitled "My Political Philosophy", which was published in the September edition of the Japanese magazine *Voice*. The essay was all the more remarkable since the DPJ had been elected only weeks before on a manifesto that advocated entering negotiations for a Japan-U.S. FTA.

[38] Hatoyama Yukio, "A New Path for Japan," *New York Times*, August 27, 2009. https://www.nytimes.com/2009/08/27/opinion/27iht-edhatoyama.html?_r=1&pagewanted=print.

[39] Hatoyama, "A New Path for Japan."

[40] The Meiji era was from 1868 until 1912, and the Taishō era from 1912 until 1926.

[41] Quoted in de Bary et al. (2010).

[42] The original piece was published in Japanese in the print version of the newspaper and on the *Asahi* website. The version quoted here appeared in translation on the newspaper's English-language website.

[43] Asahi Shimbun, "Concern in the Country of Rice Plants."

[44] Asahi Shimbun, "Concern in the Country of Rice Plants."

[45] Mark Blyth (1997, 231) has argued that ideas were added on as variables to address shortcomings in both rational choice and historical institutionalist approaches, and that one's understanding of institutions shape one's conception of ideas and what they do, and vice verse. Rational institutionalists who see ideas as contractual arrangements between individuals will see ideas as 'functional devices' manipulated by individuals in pursuit of their interests. Historical institutionalists who see ideas as world-views come to see institutions as 'situated practices' or 'standard operating procedures.'

[46] Thies (1998) offers a rational institutionalist account of Japan's agricultural protectionism as a comparative study with the United States that does not include an ideational dimension. Among several contestable claims, Thies contends that agricultural support and protection waned in Japan from about 1980 after members from urban constituencies became the majority in the LDP, and that the courts rectified Japan's electoral malapportionment.

[47] In this account, "unsuccessful efforts by state officials to respond to policy failures and anomalies in the existing paradigm eventually trigger a broader, societal, political partisan debate about policy principles. From this society-wide contestation over policy goals, problems, and solutions, a new policy paradigm emerges." (Coleman et al., 1997, 273)

[48] Sheingate (2000, 2001) offers a historical institutionalist account of Japanese agricultural policy as a comparative case study with the United States and France, but does not consider ideational factors.

[49] A number of debates about the precise role of the media exist, such as whether and how the media directly influence politicians to set the political agenda, whether politicians take the media as a proxy for public opinion, and whether politicians themselves use the media to influence public opinion. In the present model, the media is considered primarily in terms of its role as a vector for ideas.

[50] Ashizawa's value-action framework holds that *identities* shape values, which in turn shape preferences, which shape policies. The actors are state agents making foreign policy. The current model is different in that it takes *ideas* as shaping values, individuals as the actors, and deals with preferences to domestic (agricultural) policies. The current model is applicable not just to policymakers but to all

individuals in a society. Whereas this approach when applied to policymakers would result in actual policies being made, implemented, or continued, when applied to all individuals in a society (who lack policy-making capacity), the result is preference for a given policy.

[51] Such factors would include electoral systems, election turnout, restrictive electoral participation laws, and electoral district malapportionment, among others.

[52] Banzan and Sorai are here referred to by the names by which they are commonly known.

[53] Satō's state-centred writings subsequently inspired ultranationalists in the 1930s.

[54] Also known as Ninomiya Kinjirō.

[55] Also known as Tani Tateki.

[56] The two strands were formerly classed separately by historians, but subsequently the similarities between the two movements were emphasised, particularly in terms of the role of "middling" farmers (Waswo, 1989: 558, 559).

[57] Also known as Gondō Seikei or Gondō Narikuni.

[58] Sometimes written as Tachibana Kōsaburō.

[59] For example, Ogura (1980) cites the agriculture ministry consultant Max Fesca, the Imperial university professor Udo Eggert, and Satō Shōsuke as advocates of more market-based large-scale or mixed-scale farming in the late 1800s.

[60] The policy measures stipulated by the Supreme Commander of the Allied Powers (SCAP) in the agrarian reform directive of December 1945 included land transfers from absentee owners to land operators, provisions for tenants to purchase land at reasonable rates, protection against reversion to tenancy status, access to credit at reasonable rates, measures against exploitation by processors and distributors, price stabilisation measures, provision of technical assistance, and the fostering of "an agricultural cooperative movement free of domination by non-agrarian interests and dedicated to the economic and cultural advancement of the Japanese farmer" (quoted in de Bary et al, 2010).

[61] Those employed in agriculture dropped from 16.1 million in 1950 to 13.1 million in 1960 and would fall again to 9.3 million by 1970 (Kosai, 1989, 502).

[62] In terms of achieving income parity for farmers with respect to urban workers, the 1961 framework was more than successful, with the farmer-to-worker income ratio rising from 0.92 in 1960 to 1.39 in 1975 and 1.23 in 2000. However, the majority of farmers' total income came from non-farm sources as farming became a side-job for many, such that farm income represented only about 1/8 of total farmer income by 2000 (see Yamashita, 2014, 70).

[63] Mulgan (2006, 116-7) argues that the law combined deregulatory and market reform aspects with the entrenchment of agricultural intervention, as evidenced by "dichotomous pairs of ideas" listed in the text of the law: "reform and protection (*kaikaku to hozen*), competition and co-existence (*kyōsō to kyōsei*), the market and the state (*shijō to seifu*), and globalism and nationalism (*gurōbaruisumu to nashonarizumu*)."

[64] There is a fifth national daily newspaper in Japan, the *Sankei Shimbun*, which has a smaller daily circulation than the other papers, and sits quite far to the right of the political spectrum. This newspaper was omitted from the analysis due to its more hardline editorial position, and to the fact that the four papers selected represented a balanced spread of positions on the political spectrum.
[65] It is important to note that the political spectrum in Japan does not conform neatly to the Western model of left and right, but the convention is employed here to give a rough idea of alignment.
[66] Such sales figures are likely boosted by the common practice of bulk purchases of newspapers by businesses, offices, hotels, and other entities.
[67] "Newspaper Circulation in Japan: Still High but Steadily Falling." *Nippon.com*, December 5, 2014. http://www.nippon.com/en/features/h00084/.
[68] Some also have their own sub-fields of economics, like the environment and health.
[69] Inevitably, a degree of subjective judgement was required in the framing analysis. To ensure replicability, a second coder also analysed the articles independently.
[70] *93rd Statistical Yearbook*, Section 3-2-9.
[71] *Nihon Seisaku Kinyū Kōko* [Japan Finance Company], 5 August 2020, https://www.jfc.go.jp/n/findings/pdf/topics_200805a.pdf
[72] "Safe Food for Japan," *New York Times*, 11 October 2007. https://www.nytimes.com/2007/10/11/business/worldbusiness/11safety.html
[73] Other Cabinet Office surveys also touched on issues relating to agriculture or food in ways that were not germane to the present study, such as surveys about food rationing in the 1950s or general eating habits in more recent years. No survey since 2014 has focused on agriculture and food.
[74] The survey themes covered a range of topics connected to agriculture, food, and rural society, and the precise questions often varied. Even in the case where the same questions were asked in successive years, the wording of questions were sometimes changed. What is presented here is a summary that draws together questions that were identical, similar or on the same theme, such that they can be compared over a long time-frame.
[75] I am grateful to my Japanese colleagues who aided with the preparation of the questions.
[76] According to the historian John Dower, though the imperial throne was strongly supported by SCAP and leading Japanese politicians, and postwar polls also indicated widespread popular support, other evidence suggested a more ambivalent public attitude to the emperor in this period (Dower, 1999, 298, 302).
[77] There were 408 responses to this question. Consistent with other results reported in this chapter, responses are shown as percentages of the total sample of 500.
[78] Abe's first term in office was from September 2006 until September 2007, when he resigned for health reasons.

[79] MAFF, "'Seme no nōrinsuisangyō' no jitsugen ni mukete" [Towards the realisation of 'Agriculture, Forestry and Fisheries on the Offensive], May 2014, https://www.kantei.go.jp/jp/singi/keizaisaisei/kadaibetu/dai3/siryou3.pdf.

[80] The 'sixth' sector derived from adding (or multiplying) the numerals of the primary, secondary and tertiary sectors.

[81] James Brady, "The Yabu Special Zone: An incipient model for agricultural reform and rural revitalisation." *Asia Pacific Institute of Research*, Commentary No. 54, December 18, 2015.
https://www.apir.or.jp/wp/wp-content/uploads/APIR_Commentary_No542.pdf

[82] Yamashita Kazuhito, "No More of the False Report of Abolition of the Gentan Policy!", Canon Institute for Global Studies, May 18, 2018.
https://cigs.canon/en/article/20180601_5072.html.

[83] Yamashita Kazuhito, "Discord emerging in the agricultural policy triangle of the JA, norinzoku and the farm ministry." *Canon Institute of Global Studies,* April 16, 2020. https://cigs.canon/en/article/20200416_6338.html.

[84] Kantei [Prime Minister's Office], "Economic Policy Speech by H.E. Mr. Shinzo Abe, Prime Minister of Japan." Guildhall, City of London, June 19, 2013.
http://japan.kantei.go.jp/96_abe/statement/201306/19guildhall_e.html.

[85] Yamashita Kazuhito, "A First Step Toward Reform of Japan's Agricultural Cooperative System." *Nippon.com*, April 20, 2015.
https://www.nippon.com/en/currents/d00169/a-first-step-toward-reform-of-japan's-agricultural-cooperative-system.html

[86] "Food security exists when all people, at all times, have physical, social and economic access to sufficient, safe and nutritious food which meets their dietary needs and food preferences for an active and healthy life." "Food Security Statistics," FAO. http://www.fao.org/economic/ess/ess-fs/en/

[87] "Coronavirus disease (COVID-19) pandemic," World Health Organisation.
https://www.who.int/emergencies/diseases/novel-coronavirus-2019.

[88] "Quarterly GDP (indicator)." OECD, accessed September 12, 2020.
doi: 10.1787/b86d1fc8-en

[89] "Food Supply Chains and COVID-19: Impacts and Policy Lessons." *OECD*, June 2, 2020. http://www.oecd.org/coronavirus/policy-responses/food-supply-chains-and-covid-19-impacts-and-policy-lessons-71b57aea/.

[90] Stephens, Emma C., et al, "Editorial: Impacts of COVID-19 on agricultural and food systems worldwide and on progress to the sustainable development goals." *National Institutes of Health*, August 2020.
https://www.ncbi.nlm.nih.gov/pmc/articles/PMC7237936/

[91] "Q&A: COVID-19 Pandemic - impact on food and agriculture," FAO,
http://www.fao.org/2019-ncov/q-and-a/impact-on-food-and-agriculture/en/

[92] "COVID-19 Impacts on Food Distribution in Japan," USDA Report Number JA2020-0076, April 9, 2020. https://bit.ly/3isSBGA

[93] "Etō Nōrinsuisan Daijin Kisha Kaiken Gaiyō [Outline of the Press Conference by the Agriculture, Forestry and Fisheries Minister Eto]," *MAFF*, April 14, 2020. https://www.maff.go.jp/j/press-conf/200414.html.
[94] Yamashita Kazuhito, "The reason why the stupid plan of 'wagyu gift certificates' was proposed." *Canon Institute for Global Studies*, May 8, 2020. https://cigs.canon/en/article/20200508_6381.html
[95] "Korona go mo Osō Sekaiteki 'Shokuryō Kiki' no Shizuka na Tōrai" [Even after Coronavirus, a Quiet Global Food Crisis Attack is Coming]. Tōyō Keizai, 15 May 2020. toyokeizai.net/articles/-/350134.
[96] "Trade Statistics Data for Japan," *e-Stat: Portal Site of Official Statistics of Japan.* https://www.e-stat.go.jp/en/stat-search/files?page=1&toukei=00350300&tstat=000001013141
[97] "Update: COVID-19 Among Workers in Meat and Poultry Processing Facilities — United States, April–May 2020," *Centers for Disease Control and Prevention.* https://www.cdc.gov/mmwr/volumes/69/wr/mm6927e2.htm.
[98] Tōyō Keizai, May 15, 2020.
[99] Yamashita Kazuhito, "Grain prices will suffer a slump in tandem with crude oil due to the coronavirus crisis," *Canon Institute for Global Studies*, June 1, 2020. https://cigs.canon/en/article/20200601_6449.html.
[100] "Shingata Koronauirusu kansenshō ni tsuite" [Concerning the novel coronavirus infection], *MAFF*, https://www.maff.go.jp/j/saigai/n_coronavirus/index.html#c00.
[101] "Climate Change and Agriculture. A Perfect Storm in Farm Country." *Union of Concerned Scientists*, March 20, 2019. www.ucsusa.org/resources/climate-change-and-agriculture
[102] "Land & Water: Land assessment and impacts," *FAO*. http://www.fao.org/land-water/land/land-assessment/en/.
[103] "Growing at a slower pace, works population is expected to reach 9.7 billion in 2050, and could peak at nearly 11 billion around 2100." *United Nations Department of Economic and Social Affairs*, June 17, 2019. www.un.org/development/desa/en/news/population/world-population-prospects-2019.html
[104] "Japan braces for further damage by crop-hungry fall armyworm." *Kyodo News,* August 15, 2020. https://english.kyodonews.net/news/2020/08/d1aa25a18723-japan-braces-for-further-damage-by-crop-hungry-fall-armyworm.html.
[105] Shiotsu Fumitaka, "Japan has outstanding agricultural technologies to combat climate change; will it help the world?", *Meiji University*, August 9, 2018. https://www.meiji.ac.jp/cip/english/research/opinion/Fumitaka_Shiotsu.html
[106] "Population Projections for Japan (2016-2065): Summary." *Institute of Population and Social Security Research.* http://www.ipss.go.jp/pp-zenkoku/e/zenkoku_e2017/pp_zenkoku2017e_gaiyou.html

[107] "Food Poisoning Statistics 2009." *Ministry of Health, Labour and Welfare.* https://www.mhlw.go.jp/english/topics/foodsafety/poisoning/dl/Food_Poisoning_Statistics_2009.pdf

[108] "Raw beef liver ban had little impact on E. coli in Japan." *Food Safety News*, December 26, 2019. https://www.foodsafetynews.com/2019/12/raw-beef-liver-ban-had-little-impact-on-e-coli-in-japan/.

[109]"Fukushima Daiichi Status Updates—17 July 2020," *International Atomic Energy Agency.* https://www.iaea.org/newscenter/focus/fukushima/status-update.

[110] "List of countries and regions that have lifted import measures on Japanese food imposed after the TEPCO's Fukushima Daiichi Nuclear Power Plant accident." *MAFF*, May 20, 2020.
https://www.maff.go.jp/j/export/e_info/pdf/kisei_keii_en.pdf.

[111] Cabinet Office, "Kokumin Seikatsu ni kan suru Seron Chōsa" [Public Opinion Survey on the Life of Citizens]. June 2012. https://survey.gov-online.go.jp/h24/h24-life/3_chosahyo.html

[112] Cabinet Office, "Shoku to Nōringyogyō ni kan suru Chishiki, Keihatsu, Jōhō Teikyō Seron Chōsa" [Public Opinion Survey on Knowledge Diffusion, Understanding and Information Supply regarding Food and the Agriculture, Forestry and Fisheries Sectors]. September 2018. https://survey.gov-online.go.jp/h30/h30-shoku/3_chosahyo.html

[113] Yamashita Kazuhito, "The pandemic is unlikely to cause a food crisis," *Canon Institute for Global Studies*, May 26, 2020.
https://cigs.canon/en/article/20200605_6465.html

[114] "Nōchi no mitōshi to kakuho" [Outlook for and securing of Agricultural Land]." *MAFF*, Basic Plan for Agriculture, Food, and Forestry, March 2020.
https://www.maff.go.jp/j/keikaku/k_aratana/attach/pdf/index-8.pdf

[115] Yamashita," Discord emerging in the agricultural policy triangle."

[116] Rausch, Anthony, "Akiya Bank: A Solution To Japan's 'Abandoned 'Homes?" *Tokyo Review*, April 28, 2020. https://www.tokyoreview.net/2020/04/akiya-bank-japan-abandoned-homes/.

INDEX